HOW TO ART

ALSO BY KATE BRYAN

The Art of Love
Bright Stars

How to Art

Bringing a Fancy Subject Down to Earth

KATE BRYAN

with illustrations by David Shrigley

WORKMAN PUBLISHING · NEW YORK

Workman
Workman Publishing
Hachette Book Group, Inc.
1290 Avenue of the Americas
New York, NY 10104
workman.com

Workman is an imprint of Workman Publishing, a division of Hachette Book Group, Inc.
The Workman name and logo are registered trademarks of Hachette Book Group, Inc.

Originally published in September 2025 by Penguin Random House UK

Set in 12.5/16pt Adobe Caslon Pro
Typeset by Jouve (UK), Milton Keynes
Cover illustration by David Shrigley

The publisher is not responsible for websites (or their content) that are not owned
by the publisher.

Workman books may be purchased in bulk for business, educational, or promotional use.
For information, please contact your local bookseller or the Hachette Book Group Special
Markets Department at special.markets@hbgusa.com.

Library of Congress Cataloging-in-Publication Data is available.

ISBN 978-1-5235-3418-0

First Edition September 2025

Printed in China APO on responsibly sourced paper.

10 9 8 7 6 5 4 3 2 1

To my beautiful parents, Gary and Julie Soden.
I love you and your creativity.
(I'm the middle one.)

CONTENTS

And Three Useful Things

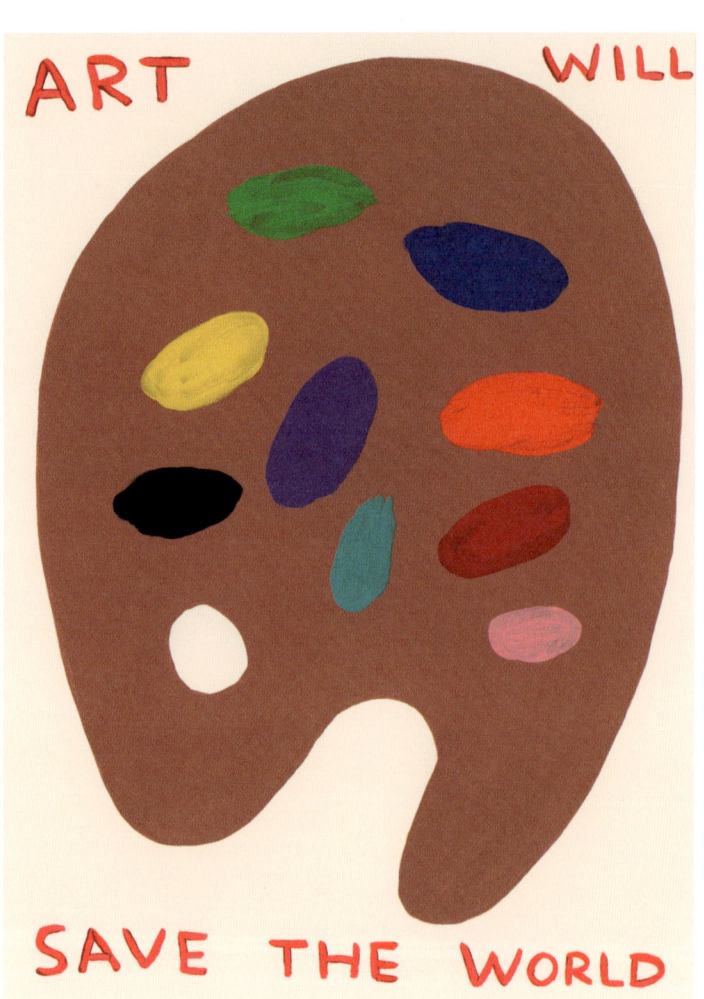

INTRODUCTION : WHY ART?

I believe art is for everybody. Art is universal and it does not discriminate. It is a language without words and a means of sharing our most important and beautiful ideas with one another. So, when I say art is for everybody, I mean *everybody*. You don't need to study it, or to make a career creating it, or to have grown up in a mansion stuffed with artworks for it to be meaningful to you.

For too long art has been treated as an exclusive field, with vast numbers of us feeling like we're on the outside looking in – or worse still, turning away altogether out of intimidation, frustration, or both. A collective art anxiety has developed: it's as if art has been stolen away and placed in a room only available to those with the right access codes. But art is intrinsic to all of us. Whether it's a child's drawing pinned on the fridge, a painting in a chapel, an ancient sculpture, a handprint on a cave wall, or a show in a gallery, art has always been an inherent part of human culture and history. Its threads connect people the world over, bringing us the same wonder and joy as music, providing the same comfort as good food, allowing us the liberty of dance, taking us out of our everyday lives to think about the bigger picture in the same way as philosophy.

I did not grow up in a rarefied world. I went to a local comprehensive school and in a pre-internet age I did what everyone else did: played until dark in the street with my siblings and my neighbours, listened to CDs with my mates, doodled over every schoolbook, and watched Tony Hart, the UK equivalent of Bob Ross on the telly. I made art all the time, and slowly through a few good books I found myself soaking up famous artworks. I discovered a whole new way of looking at and understanding the world through this art and the artists who made it. I've now spent over half my life thinking about, looking at, and talking about art, and I am certain that it's made me more receptive to the thoughts, feelings, creative impulses, and experiences of people I might never meet – ancient and contemporary alike. To me, it's not just a pity but a crying shame that so many of us are missing out on this through no fault of our own. One of my main motivations for writing this book is how often people say to me something along the lines of, 'I don't know anything about art, but I do like David Hockney.' But no one is diminishing themselves by saying, 'I don't know anything about music, but I love Coldplay.'

Global visitor numbers for the top 100 museums in the world are in the hundreds of millions.* Even so, there is still a nervousness about the 'proper' way to respond to what we see when we are in these spaces. I'm hoping that some of what follows can allow for our natural instincts to shine through, to help you own and

---

*Cheshire, L., and da Silva, J. (2024), 'The 100 most popular art museums in the world – blockbusters, bots and bounce-backs', *The Arts Newspaper*, www.theartnews paper.com/2024/03/26/the-100-most-popular-art-museums-in-the-world-2023

develop your interest in the things that excite you and walk away without guilt from those works that don't.

After making it through university (I studied Art History), I started working at the British Museum, where I often felt completely out of place. I had zero connections to people already in the field, and no points of reference for how to be, day to day, when working in the art world. (I remember being asked a few times, 'What does your father do?' and replying 'When?', while thinking, *What does he do when? When he wakes up?*) I spent the next few years learning how to fit in. In truth, I suppose I essentially learned how and when to hide my working-class background. I learned the rules of the game and believed that if people wanted to have a relationship to art they could, like me, study it, become well versed in art history, and learn how to talk about it in the same way as the people already in the room. I find this acutely embarrassing to think about now, but I confess it because I think it remains a dominant belief: one ought to know an awful lot about art to talk about art.

Now though, I know that even if we gave those with art anxiety the time, money, and inclination to devote themselves to an art education, we'd still be missing the point. The point is to unlock the stuff that's already inside us. Not only is it completely unacceptable to expect everyone to 'level up' to meet the demands and rigour of the art world's systems, but also we can reveal these systems to be non-essential.

This book, therefore, hopes to be the key that cracks the codes, a secret map that guides us through the rooms, a guide to what we might find when we're there – and an encouragement to carry the stuff back to enjoy in our own homes. It's a call to arms, an invitation – and, I hope, a shortcut – to bring art into your life. Although we may feel like it, none of us are strangers to art; as children we all made it for years. It is a fundamental and natural impulse to make and look at art. Somehow our right to it, our innate language around it, got separated from us, and it's time to take it back. We should be able to access and enjoy art as easily as we do music or food without first obtaining some sort of certificate of authority.

Therefore, *How to Art* offers you art to enjoy while you read. As we take this journey, you'll see specially made artworks by my friend and fellow campaigner for the wellbeing that art can deliver us, the internationally respected and beloved David Shrigley. His art is brilliant, full of wit, verve, and essential truths. We hope that this book is as fun, straightforward, and comforting as the art world can seem pretentious, fancy, and intimidating.

Along with artworks from David, what follows aims to arm you with the tools to find, build, and sustain a meaningful and life-affirming relationship with art. I'm not here to provide a dumbed-down version of what people learn at university or art school. Formally studying art is a completely valid route into art (and one I followed) but it's not the only way. The approach in *How to Art* is to provide simple strategies that might aid you wherever you may be and whoever you are – whether you're a seasoned art-lover, a sometimes-visitor keen to see a famous artwork on holiday, an artist yourself, or a total newbie. Although it might seem a little unusual for one book to aim to appeal to both professional artists and those who have never stepped foot inside a gallery, I've chosen to take a 360-degree approach because to my mind this is an important part of demystifying art.

The book begins in Part One by working out where to find this stuff called art, how art spaces operate, and what you can expect when you're in them. And then it goes deeper by tackling an important but often-ignored question: what is art? To reach a conclusion we take a speedy gambol from the earliest recorded art through to things people might accuse of being 'the emperor's new clothes'.

In Part Two, I zoom in on looking at art and talking about it. And good news for the more sceptical reader: as well as articulating what we like, we get to talk about what we *don't* like because, and I hope this is a relief to hear, you will not – and should not – like all art. I also tackle how to enjoy art with small children in tow. As someone with plenty of first-hand experience of this, I give to you my tried-and-tested formula of how to go to a gallery with kids (which I also once used successfully with my older brother when we were in our thirties). And because I am serious about art being for everybody, even those with four legs, I complement this with a not-entirely-daft interlude on how to make your dog more cultural. And although I want you to feel empowered to pass on art that does nothing for you, I'd love it if Michelangelo's Sistine Chapel ceiling, Leonardo's *Mona Lisa*, and van Gogh's *Sunflowers* had a fighting chance. They are works of such staggering fame and touristic appeal that their primary function – as works of art intended to move us – is sometimes obscured. I present them to you again as examples of how to turn the noise down around famous artworks and allow yourself to enter the picture. This section ends with how to experience art at home with an emphasis on entertainment and pleasure as opposed to education.

Part Three focuses on why we should all be making art – even me, an experienced television broadcaster and established art curator who technically invites career suicide every time I pick up a paintbrush only for it to do nothing that I want it to do. I reassure myself that a great food critic can't cook like the supreme chefs she reviews, yet she can still enjoy trying to make herself a half-decent plate of food every now and again. Like taking time to cook for yourself, making art is absurdly good for us, and I want to help you to quiet your inner critic, try out drawing for beginners, and make art a social event.

Part Four takes things up a notch by looking at owning your own art. I find this area really exciting: there has never been an easier and more rewarding time to buy art for yourself, and the benefits can be exceptional. I start by explaining why I think regular people can and should buy art. We then look at how to get your eye in, how art is priced, and where to find inexpensive art, before moving on to more specific advice about surviving art fairs. I also discuss how to make art look amazing in your home, including advice on framing art, hanging a salon wall, and caring for your art.

Part Five, the final section, talks to and about those who are artists, whether they're just beginning or have many years of experience, with advice from the book's resident artist, David Shrigley. It looks at how artists actually make a living, how to stay motivated, and practical matters that I know many artists struggle with, such as writing an artist statement. Non-artists might find it interesting as an insight into the kind of problems and worries artists have to deal with in service of making their work. Finally, I hope that it might help everybody to learn how to think and see the world more like artists do: finding beauty and marvels in the everyday, transforming matter into magic, and creating objects that can speak across time and space.

So, let's dive in. The water's lovely.

Kate

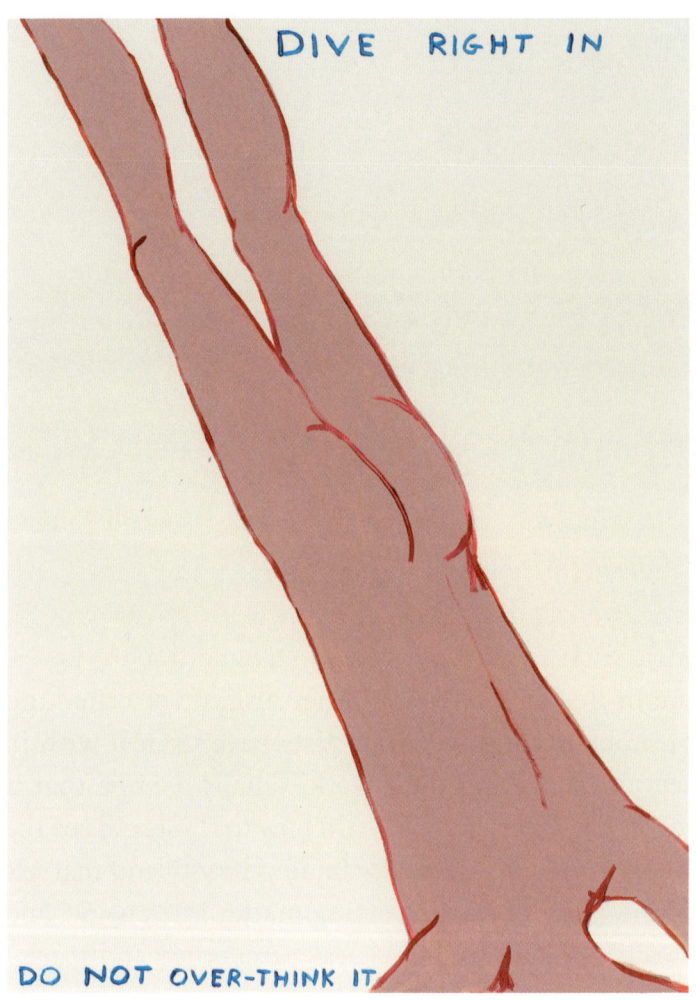

PART ONE:
HOW TO FIND ART AND THINK ABOUT WHAT ART CAN BE

HOW TO FIND ART

Sometimes I like to shock people in the art world, and it's absurdly easy. All I have to do is say the following: 'Before I entered the art world, I had only seen artworks in galleries twice.'

I didn't live on a remote Scottish island – in fact I grew up only an hour from London by train – nor did I have any physical impairments that might be barriers to access. I just didn't know anyone who talked about art, owned art, or visited museums. I wasn't related to anyone who'd gone to university, I didn't have much money for train fares, and I didn't know that public museums in the UK are free. Even if I had known that, I wouldn't have known where to begin. Crucially, I was not remotely unusual in this regard – vast numbers of people were, and are, in a similar situation.

Talking about my experience often raises eyebrows in the art world though because most people working in auction houses, art galleries, major museums, and cultural organisations have mixed with many art-educated people, visited countless museums in multiple countries, and had a first-class education. I didn't know it at the time, but my passion for art – born from hours painting and looking at pictures in a few art books – was leading me blindly into an elite crowd.

In contrast to this art-savvy bunch, the sum total of my real-world art experience before university was one school trip to the Tate in the early nineties, where I bought a postcard of Matisse's marvellously inventive *Snail*, and one visit with my parents to see a Monet exhibition at the Royal Academy in 1999 to celebrate my seventeenth birthday. I still remember seeing Monet's sublimely beautiful paintings in those enormous historic rooms and suddenly realising that it was someone's job to put them there. I eyed the security guards with envy: they were being paid to watch Monet's paintings, whereas at that time I was being paid to watch grim beef patties roll through the broiler at Burger King.

I may only have been in the same room as important art twice, but these experiences were plenty enough for me to apply to study for an undergraduate degree in Art History at the University of Warwick, which in itself was a bit of a fluke. I had never heard the words 'art' and 'history' used together until I visited a further education fair at the University of Reading. In neat rows of gazebos across the lawn there were presentations for each subject arranged alphabetically. I started with English and then found my way to History, only for my jaw to drop, in what remains one of my most vivid and still-electric memories. Next to History was History of Art. 'What is the history of art?' I asked, a question that changed everything for me. I wish I could tell you how the person minding the gazebo answered, but I can't remember – my mind was already filling in all the blanks. As a concept, the idea that art is a valid and worthwhile way to understand the world made complete sense to me.

Because I already had a relationship to art. I might never have met an artist, I might only have been to the Tate once, but art was something that I had an easy and natural affinity with. I made art almost every day and spent a lot of time looking at reproductions of it in books. I can easily bring to mind the artists that I spent so much time with as a teenager: Vincent van Gogh, Andy Warhol, Georgia O'Keeffe, and Claude Monet were my crew. I only had a few books, but they were well worn; I would look at them over and over again. (I still 'own' a couple of the books, which I realise now might make them Wokingham Library's longest ever 'loan'. You know where to find me if you need them back.)

I say all this because, without having seen everything I have now seen (and read and published and acquired), I was still completely valid in describing myself back then as someone who loved art. Don't think you need to spend all your time, money, and energy cultivating an enormous footprint in museums and galleries or reading art historical tomes before you are allowed to 'belong' in the art world or to talk about or make art. I was already worthy, and *you* are already worthy.

Sitting here, picturing my seventeen-year-old self and marvelling at the purity of my attraction to art, I know

I would have found *some* direction on how and where I could love art immensely useful. I was addicted to this stuff – I wanted more of it! So, what follows is an introduction to where you might find art at home and further afield. Remember: this art is not going anywhere, so there's no desperate rush to see everything. Furthermore, you don't have to like all of what you see – in fact I'd actively encourage you not to, but more on that later.

NATIONAL MUSEUMS AND GALLERIES - HOME TO THE 'CANON'

First off, a small note on the words 'museum' and 'gallery'. A lot of people think art (like a Frida Kahlo painting) is in galleries, whereas historical objects (like an Egyptian mummy) are in museums. But the words are used interchangeably, with both used by organisations that hold and display artworks. So, rather than try and distinguish between museums and galleries when it comes to art, I'm simply going to talk about what's in them instead.

National museums and national galleries, which are usually found in capital cities, are two (contradictory) things at once. They are both slightly elite in that they only show the best of the best, but also very accessible – not just because they are so famous that they are easy to find, but also because in many parts of the world they are free or subsidised for locals. The Metropolitan Museum of Art in New York, for example, is 'Pay As

You Wish' for residents of New York state and students from New York, New Jersey, and Connecticut. Washington DC is home to many major museums, such as the National Museum of African American History and Culture, the National Portrait Gallery, and the National Gallery of Art, all of which are free to visit. As already mentioned, it is standard practice that the permanent collections in all national museums in the UK are free to enter – there would actually need to be a change in the law to allow them to charge. The British Museum has been free since it opened in 1759, and so has the National Gallery since it opened just over 200 years ago. In the UK we call these 'public' institutions because they are for the public, don't make any commercial profit, and report to the government. Nothing is for sale, nothing has a price tag, and everything is staying put for centuries. Think of these institutions as custodians of something that the public collectively owns: these are the nation's collections and there are millions of artworks in them. Most temporary exhibitions (those that bring together a group of works for a set length of time, usually on loan from other museums or private collections) have to be paid for, but there are exceptions and reduced prices for children, students, elderly people, people on low incomes, and people with disabilities.

When you visit these national museums and galleries, you are seeing what is referred to as the 'art historical canon' (which I always say in my best serious, deep voice), which means works by artists that have been revered and respected for a long time and make up the stepping stones of art throughout history – artists like Leonardo, Rembrandt, Picasso, and Warhol. When I was finishing university back in 2003, it felt like that canon was set in stone. It didn't seem like anyone was going to go back to add in artists who'd been over-looked, and the prevailing thought was that there wasn't much to be done about the fact that the canon was almost exclusively a white men's club. I didn't go to university in Victorian Britain, but nonetheless we were not taught about artists of colour or queer art and I studied only a handful of women artists and even they were only discussed on a specialist feminist art course. It was then that I discovered the Guerrilla Girls – anonymous masked crusaders who label themselves 'the conscience of the art world', creating punchy and witty statistics-based posters that call attention to systemic sexism and racism in art and beyond.

Thanks to this kind of art activism, it feels like in the last two decades the tectonic plates upon which the canon sits are actually beginning to shift. This is not about throwing out the great talents who have always lined the hallowed halls of national museums. Monet will always be a household name, but now we are also talking about Berthe Morisot, a female Impressionist and key figure of this period. Why is this important? Well, if art is a means for us humans to speak to each other in ways that defy the limitations of geography and time, we are only getting a sliver of the full picture of who we are if one set of artists with a similar world view is doing all the talking. Furthermore, we risk alienating audiences and losing vital stories that inspire, warn, and instruct us.

In national museums and galleries there is a long way to go to put more people in the historical record. A 2019 study of eighteen major US museums showed that 85 per cent of artists in their collections are white and 87 per cent are male.* The National Gallery, on Trafalgar Square in London, has a collection that ends in the year 1900. Just 1 per cent of the artists in its collection are women, and they first exhibited an artist of colour, Jan Toorop, in their permanent galleries in 2023. Tate Modern on the other hand, who can regularly acquire work from living artists because their collection begins in 1900 and has no cut-off date, is able to boast that nearly 40 per cent of the artists on display are women, and is making deep inroads to diversify who is represented on its walls. Changing what makes up the collection and who comes to see it is a huge part of the puzzle in making art more democratic.

REGIONAL ART MUSEUMS

The USA boasts the highest number of art museums in the world. What makes it so unique is that art museums are found across the entire country, not just in more obvious large cities like New York or

* Topaz, C. M., et al. (2019), 'Diversity of artists in major US museums', *PLoS One* 14(3): e0212852.

Washington DC – there are nearly 700 university art museums alone. This is important, because spending time with art should not require having to travel enormous distances or making it into a touristic endeavour. Italy is also incredibly fortunate in this respect: there is so much medieval and Renaissance artwork in situ in churches, so across the country people live in close proximity to important artwork. In the UK, you might assume that all the major art museums are in London. However, there are important and sizeable public collections elsewhere too. Regional museums sometimes overlap with national museums. The Tate, for example, is a national museum with two locations in London (Tate Modern and Tate Britain) but also two locations outside London, Tate Liverpool and Tate St Ives. Each province and territory of Canada maintains a museum with pieces mainly from that territory but also beyond and there are also large public art galleries in many of the cities like the Vancouver Art Gallery or the Art Gallery of Ontario in Toronto.

LOCAL PUBLIC ART GALLERIES

The difference between national and regional art museums and what I am calling local public art galleries is that the latter are more modestly sized, sometimes with focused collections – like the Estorick in North London, which only shows modern Italian art. Local public art galleries are often a collection that belonged to a private individual that then became a museum after their death. This means that they are often esoteric, and you get the sense that the gallery has a distinct personality. Generally speaking, these galleries are not where you go to see nothing but masterpieces; instead, they are great place to find unusual artworks and names that might otherwise have been forgotten, all held together by the collecting habits of one individual, such as the Isabella Stewart Gardner Museum in Boston. In some cases, these museums are the former home of an artist, such as Gainsborough's House in Suffolk, Casa Buonarroti (formerly owned by Michelangelo) in Florence, and the Frida Kahlo Museum in Mexico City.

In the past couple of decades, there has been a push to use culture to help to revitalise neglected towns and cities. For example, the opening of public contemporary art institutions in seaside towns such as Margate (the Turner Contemporary), Hastings (the Hastings Contemporary), Portsmouth (the Box Gallery), and Eastbourne (the Towner) was connected to local authority regeneration programmes and consequently attracted a lot of artists to relocate to these areas. In this fashion, in the USA some contemporary artists are making community-driven art projects very much part of their art practice, such as Chicago-based art-world superstar Theaster Gates. With a background in city planning, Gates deftly weaves together art and urban-regeneration initiatives, such as Stony Island Arts Bank, a derelict bank in Chicago's South Side turned into an art gallery, community space, and archive. Likewise, Los Angeles-based Mark Bradford put his socially minded art into action with Art + Practice, which consists of a gallery, art studio space, lecture and film theatres, and educational resources, bringing a vibrant cultural hub into a long-underserved neighbourhood. These forward-thinking artists and those who are following suit send a strong message about what art spaces can achieve and how vital they are as places of community, education, and solace.

PRIVATE MUSEUMS - CULTURAL OFFERINGS FROM THE SUPER-RICH

Private museums are founded and operated by individuals rather than the state and usually reflect one person or family's taste and collecting habits. There has been a huge boom in private museum building, and there are now around 400 such museums across the world, from Paris to Beijing to Los Angeles to Cape Town, very often housed in pioneering spaces designed by the world's leading architects. In her 2021 book *The Rise and Rise of the Private Museum*, seasoned art market journalist Georgina Adam noted that a remarkable 70 percent of private museums devoted to contemporary art had been founded in just the past twenty years.

Private museums are designed to operate much like public ones: nothing is visibly for sale and their primary purpose is to make art available to the public – or, rather, that should be the primary purpose. However, there is ongoing speculation about the super-rich opening museums as a form of tax evasion, as reflected by the title of a 2015 *New York Times* article exposing tax benefits: 'Writing off the Warhol Next Door'. There is certainly something of an uneasy relationship between public and private museums. The latter often place less emphasis on education and community outreach, which is one of the reasons they are treated with suspicion by some people in the art world, who see them as lacking in academic rigour or even as vanity projects (let's be honest: some of them are, but you might still see something brilliant in them). But in an age of declining government funding for public museums, some argue that increased numbers of private museums should fill the gap. I think it's dangerous to assume that all private museums are somehow 'less than'. After all, many national museums started out as small private collections. For example, the collection of Sir Hans Sloane became the nucleus of the British Museum (although it should be noted that he built some of his fortune from the enslavement of people).

One of the world's largest private museums is MONA in Tasmania, Australia, which is financed by professional gambler David Walsh and has resulted in a massive tourism boom to the area since it was originally founded in 2001 (as the Moorilla Museum of Antiquities). Germany, the USA, China, and South Korea have the highest numbers of private museums in the world, but to my mind it is in Paris that the private museum has become a battlefield for a new kind of personal cultural supremacy – so much so that one could argue that the competition between two art collectors, François Pinault and Bernard Arnault, has dramatically changed the art landscape of the city in the past decade. In 2014, Arnault, the founder and CEO of the luxury conglomerate LVMH (which stands for Louis Vuitton Moët Hennessy) and one of the richest people in the world, opened the enormous Fondation Louis Vuitton, which was designed by 'starchitect' Frank Gehry and hosts jaw-dropping exhibitions of the world's greatest artists. Not to be outdone, in 2021, Pinault – founder of another luxury conglomerate, Kering, and also no stranger to seeing billions in his bank account – opened the Pinault Collection at the Bourse de Commerce in Paris, which was designed by another starchitect, Tadao Ando. Described by *Vanity Fair* in 2021 as a 'Museum-Off Between Two French Billionaires', these museums operate at the highest levels and programme some of the most remarkable exhibitions in the world.

There are over 50 private contemporary art museums in the States. Two of the most prominent are the Rubell Family Collection, which started in Miami and has a second location in Washington D.C., and The Broad in downtown Los Angeles, which offers free entry and boasts an impressive building which cost $140 million to build. The UK lags behind other countries when it comes to contemporary private museums. A couple, such as the Zabludowicz Collection and David

Roberts Art Foundation, closed their spaces in recent years, and the Saatchi Gallery is no longer home to a great collection as it was in its heyday twenty years ago and instead is more a temporary exhibition space for hire. This is a real pity, as there is such a history of great collectors giving their art to the nation such as the founders of the Wallace Collection and Sir John Soane's Museum.

London does however boast two private organisations that were recently founded by famous artists: Damien Hirst's Newport Street Gallery in Vauxhall, which shows works from his extensive personal collection, and the Gilbert and George Centre in Spitalfields, which is a shrine to the self-proclaimed 'living sculptures' Gilbert and George, who have been an artistic duo for over five decades. Both are free to visit.

COMMERCIAL ART GALLERIES – WHERE ART IS FOR SALE

Commercial galleries are where art is exhibited and sold – and so are at the opposite end of the spectrum to public art institutions, which are not for profit and are concerned with the public good. The shows in commercial galleries are temporary, with nothing consistent about your visit except the bricks and mortar you enter. The galleries represent artists like record labels do for musicians. They host and curate exhibitions of their artists' work and usually take about a 50 per cent cut of the sales – and the shows are always for sale. There is no bidding though: prices are carefully set by the gallerist and have to be adhered to.

The first commercial art gallery I stepped foot in was somewhere on New Bond Street. I was there to see a Robert Mapplethorpe exhibition, a pioneering photographer from the downtown scene of New York in the seventies and eighties. It was 2003, and I'd moved to London on the other side of my Art History degree. I'd read about this show in the exhibition review section of *Time Out* magazine, and I was delighted to read that it was free. I had to ring a doorbell to be granted entrance, and I felt completely out of place as I walked through the door. The gallery floor squeaked beneath my feet, and I assumed it was only doing so because my shoes were so cheap. I am not sure I have ever felt like such an outsider as I did then, and it makes me a bit sad even twenty years later.

I am sure Mapplethorpe would have loathed how intimidated I was. He spent a large portion of his short life broke, finding the most temporary of homes and working against the prevailing norms. He elevated photography by lavishing his subjects with such care and attention that everything he photographed – whether flowers, BDSM practices, or female bodybuilders – became exquisite somehow. He lifted everything and everyone up and was motivated to make work that spoke to the viewer, work that often shared something taboo (even flowers were taboo because they were such an old-fashioned and lowly subject at the time), but did so with the most elegant and therefore reassuring of languages. He would not have wanted people to feel excluded from his art. I don't think any artists do.

And yet most of us, even if we've heard of the private commercial galleries (like White Cube or Pace), assume that these galleries are strictly off limits to the likes of us. I felt this not only the first time I went to one, but actually also for a few years afterwards! I think it's in part because they are usually in expensive parts of a city and often have security guards at the entrance or – even more unwelcoming – the dreaded doorbell you have to ring to enter. Unlike public museums, there tends to be very little interpretation available (no wall text, individual captions for each artwork, or audio guides) and the staff working in them can seem daunting at best and sneering at worst. The ironic thing is that these galleries are completely free to visit, you don't need a ticket, and every artist showing work in these spaces would be overjoyed to find the galleries full of non-buyers.

For too long, these kinds of commercial galleries have been the preserve of the wealthy and the educated. Those with the financial means are somehow buying into this very enigmatic space, an invisible club where the status of the object transfers its lustre onto the perceived status of the collector. On my more cynical days, I might argue that commercial galleries were made purposefully obscure and unfriendly to make art seem enigmatic and unknowable, qualities that help art seem 'luxurious' and therefore very expensive. If most people are kept at a distance, or encouraged not to engage or made to feel like they can't speak any louder than a very hushed whisper in these spaces, then the art world retains all the power.

My first commercial gallery experience was not uncommon twenty years ago, but today it seems things are changing, and fast. It isn't just that I gained more confidence or learned the rules of the commercial gallery world. It's that the best of these galleries are recognising that they need to engage the public to help promote their work and/or realising that they can serve a positive societal function without destroying the allure of the art that they are selling.

One sign of these changes are the increasing numbers of 'gallery weekends' across the world (I have visited versions in Berlin, Barcelona, Rome, London, Los Angeles, and Mumbai), when galleries collectively come together in an organised fashion. There is usually a helpful map showing all the venues across the city, with galleries open for extended hours, putting on special performances, and offering a welcoming environment. You can find out about these events by simply googling 'gallery weekend' or 'gallery hop' (when galleries organise to open late on the same night, creating a kind of gallery crawl) in the city you are based in.

Another positive change is how commercial gallery buildings are being rethought. I was thrilled when White Cube opened its vast space in Bermondsey, South London, in 2011 (then the largest commercial gallery space in Europe) because there was no door bell. In fact, the gallery had a big glass sliding door, which seemed to say 'Hello, we are open, come in.' Plus there was a wheelchair-accessible public toilet and baby-changing facilities. Another fun example is Hauser & Wirth, which is a mega-gallery. With twenty-one outposts in several countries, hospitality for the general public is incorporated in Hauser & Wirth gallery spaces. In the Hauser & Wirth near Glastonbury in Somerset, they even have farm produce for sale in the cafe. A friend of mine visited it without having a clue it was a gallery that turned over tens of millions a year in art sales – she just turned up on the recommendation of a local taxi driver, who said it was family-friendly and had nice gardens. I'd love a world where all commercial galleries took a public-first approach when building their spaces, rather than seeing us as the enemy of taste.

AUCTION HOUSES - WHERE THE BIG BUCKS HAPPEN - BUT YOU CAN STILL VISIT THE ART

If I were to compare the sliding scales of perceived accessibility when visiting art to air travel, then a national gallery is economy, a commercial gallery is business class, and an auction house is first-class – or even a private jet. We think we can't get in unless we can afford to bid on the art. And yet auction houses stage exhibitions that are open to the public. Even better, these exhibitions are free and they usually display extraordinary things that will very rarely be available to view ever again, because once they are sold they tend to be put behind closed doors. So, let's rock up to the first-class lounge – because we can get in, even without a ticket.

Auction houses such as Christie's and Sotheby's – the two largest in the world, with salesrooms in cities like London, New York, Paris, and Hong Kong – sell desirable goods to the highest bidder. Although perhaps most famous for selling art, they also organise auctions for cars, memorabilia, furniture, wine, and jewels, among other things. Auction houses don't sell new works of art, like commercial galleries. They trade only in 'secondary material', which means things that have already been bought once and are now being offered for resale, usually in the hope of making a large profit.

Sales in an auction house are not selections that prioritise an artist's message above all else and are not usually curated on a theme, unless the theme is 'expensive'. Rather, sales are organised by historical period and the auction house will spend months beforehand gathering the best material and reaching out to potential buyers to get them excited and hopefully competitive. Before the big moment with the hammer and the hands in the air, there is what is known as a 'sale preview', which is basically like a museum exhibition. This is when we can all go. You don't need an appointment to visit, and there are publicly listed dates and opening hours online. No one is going to follow you around asking if you want to buy anything, though you will see some pretty serious-looking security guards.

It's in auction houses that the staggeringly high prices that occasionally make newspaper headlines (sometimes hundreds of millions of dollars) are set. There have been some incredible auction moments in recent years, such as the sale of a Leonardo da Vinci painting, *Salvator Mundi*, in 2017, which was viewed by over 27,000 people (most of whom had never stepped foot inside Christie's before) before it was sold. It was a frenzied time, when Leonardo fever gripped the public imagination, and someone was mad enough to shell out $450 million for the painting.

Artists do not make money on these auction sales, except via a relatively new financial arrangement called the 'Artist's Resale Right', which grants living artists a small percentage of the sale. At the moment the ARR is available in over 90 countries, including the EU, Britain, Australia, and Mexico, and in the U.S. it does not currently apply, but there are many who advocate for it based on the California Resale Royalty Act of 1977, which was revoked in 2018. If it were to come into effect in the U.S. it would mean that if you, say, sold a painting to your ex-landlord for $6,000 and he sold it for $1 million a few years later you would receive about $10,000 in ARR – which is at least more than the nothing you would have got for all the years up to 2006. (There are a few exceptions to this, such as Damien Hirst's sale in 2008, in which he bypassed his commercial galleries and sold new work directly at auction, which really set the cat among the pigeons because he disrupted the 'proper' way of doing things!)

It's this lack of direct reward to the maker that makes contemporary artists fairly allergic to the word 'auction'. They tend to feel that auctions exploit their work whereas the auction houses argue that it's just business. On this note, auction houses became the subject of newspaper headlines again when a work by the British street artist Banksy, who remains anonymous more than two decades into his hugely popular career, was brought for sale by Sotheby's in 2018 and started to self-destruct after the hammer went down for £1,042,000. The work entitled *Girl with Balloon* was half-shredded by a hidden device in the frame remote-controlled by Banksy – making it the first artwork to be 'created' in the auction room. It was later resold by its new owner with a revised title, *Love Is in the Bin*, in 2021 for £18,582,000 – making the original buyer a staggering profit of over £17 million. This is Banksy at his best, lampooning the art world from within and revealing the uneasy relationships that artists have with their works that quickly become mere commodities at

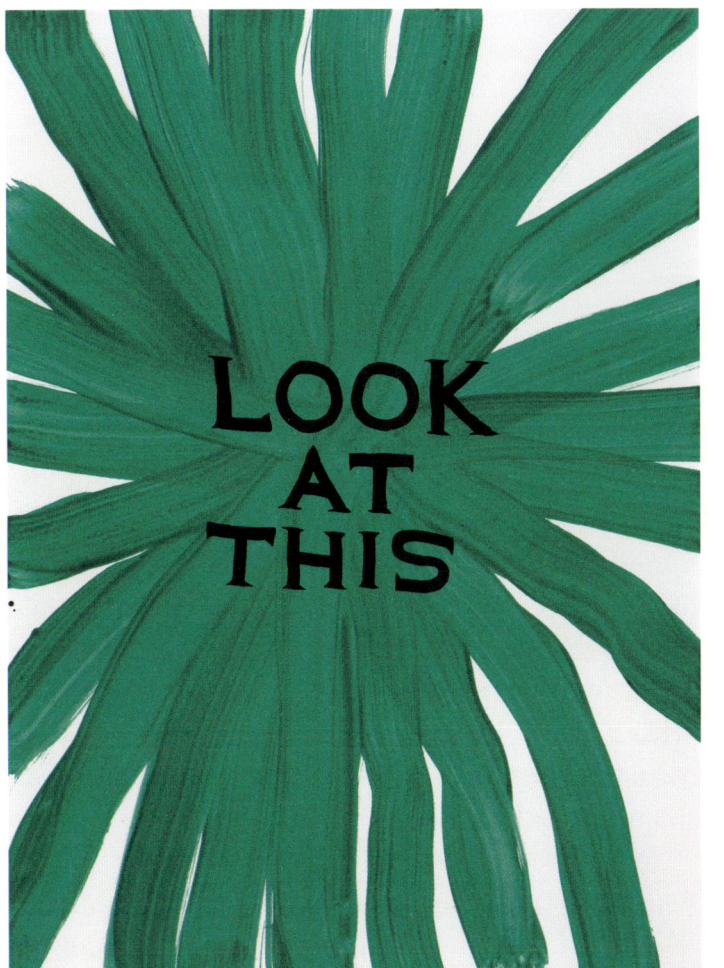

auction. The spectacle is still shrouded in mystery. How he pulled it off and whether he made any money are questions that may never be answered (trust me, I have interrogated a lot of people about this, including several who were in the room at the time!).

OPEN ARTIST STUDIOS - VISITING THE ARTIST'S SANCTUARY

It's not just professional curators – those who buy art for public institutions or museums or put on the shows at commercial galleries – who get to visit artists in their studios. The public can also gain access to these spaces through open studio initiatives. I much prefer seeing artists in their studios – something I learned to do when I started working at commercial art galleries and needed to get to know the artist and their work in more depth. A studio visit is a way to get straight to the source. Most large studio complexes host open studios once or twice a year, with organised opening hours and the artists ready to receive visitors in their private spaces. It can be really rewarding to do so, and it can even be a place to find art you want to buy (more about this on page 214).

Artists like Jenny Saville, who became the most expensive living British woman artist when her painting *Propped* (1992) sold for £9.5 million in 2018, are pretty pragmatic about auctions and quick to draw attention back to the place that matters most: the artist's studio.

'All the razzmatazz – the market, the auctions – I'm quite immune to it,' Saville has said. 'I know it's part of the process. But when you get in the studio, none of that will help you to make a better painting.'

The studio is diametrically opposed to the financial circus that is the auction house. Rather than being in public, you're definitely more at home, making it an intimate experience devoid of labels, prices, salespeople, and security guards. I love that in the studio, art is still just stuff in progress – it's not yet sanctified. Something that might one day be handled by art technicians in white gloves at Sotheby's will be propped up on the artist's filthy floor – or faced against the wall if it's a misbehaving painting in a 'time out'. In much the same way that visiting a friend in their home for the first time reveals so much about their identity, personality, history, and so on, there's something so enlightening about seeing art in the place in which it was conceived. Aside from the thrill of peeling back the curtain to see an artwork in progress, there will be materials strewn around and usually sources of inspiration such as postcards, books, and objects. These spaces are often referred to by artists as a kind of sanctuary, a place where the art is born. The Colombian artist Doris Salcedo goes even further and ascribes art in the studio with a special kind of meaning: 'When works leave my studio they no longer have anything to do with me, they become completely alien.' In colder months, it is an unwritten rule to wear multiple layers of clothing on a visit to an artist in a studio – they are, politely speaking, proper arctic.

ART FAIRS - VERY WELL-DRESSED CENTRES OF COMMERCE

Art fairs are a way of bringing lots of art into one space for sale. They usually run for less than a week. Art fairs started out much like any other trade show, but over the past thirty years they've become a huge part of the art industry, with enormous growth in the number of fairs, the number of countries that host them, the sales generated, and the number of visitors. This has occurred alongside an attempt to elevate art fairs into a cultural experience, despite the fact that most are hosted in uninspiring locations like convention centres. The two biggest companies are Art Basel, which has fairs in Basel, Miami, Hong Kong, and Paris, and Frieze, which has fairs in London, New York, Los Angeles, and Seoul. To participate in these fairs, galleries have to send detailed proposals about what they'll show, and their year-round programme has to be deemed 'serious' enough to merit a place. As well as being hard to get into, it is expensive to show at these art fairs (galleries usually pay per square metre of space and have to cover all the associated costs, such as production, shipping, installation, client events, staff travel, and accommodation). Galleries take this on the chin though, as art fairs delivers them thousands of potential clients they would not otherwise meet. That said, it's a gamble, and repeated poor performances at art fairs can lead to bankruptcy for a gallery.

It is not advisable to run a marathon without training. Obviously, this is not a book about running (I haven't run a marathon and don't plan to), but it's useful to think about the places I am suggesting you visit to look at art in a sliding scale of effort. And an art fair, well, that's your marathon. The reward will be stupendous if you feel physically, emotionally, and intellectually prepared, but it will be hard to get that much out of the experience without some kind of grounding. Start with public museums and galleries, then graduate to open studio weekends and commercial gallery shows. It's not that you need to know all the galleries and artists exhibiting at an art fair like Frieze – I don't know all that, and I go every year as a critical part of my day job. Rather, it's because it will be beneficial to build up to the stamina a fair will require, not just in terms of being on your feet (that's a consideration), but because you will see hundreds – if not thousands – of artworks in all kinds of styles and materials in a relatively small physical space, and you'll need to brace yourself for how tiring this will be.

Anyone can attend an art fair. Collectors and art-world folk get sent a VIP pass, which allows access for the duration and the preview day. Everyone else should prebook a ticket for entrance online (this is often cheaper in advance). Some fairs allow you to pay to attend the evening of the VIP day – Basel call this the Vernissage ticket. I think this is a very overrated way to go: it's upwards of £150/$200, it will be the busiest time to attend, and, make no mistake, you are not going to see Beyoncé there. Art Basel allows in kids under two for free, but charges for older ones. Frieze also charges from two years old and up and sells kids' tickets for the weekend only. Student tickets at a reduced cost are available, but book them early, as fairs don't guarantee availability.

You don't need to dress up in fancy clothes (although I would be lying if I said I didn't pre-plan all art fair outfits). However, do *not* wear uncomfortable shoes. Just don't do it to yourself. You're about to do at least 10,000 steps, so don't be a hero in Prada platforms – all the most serious collectors and museum directors will be in sneakers, because they know it's a marathon. You're also going to need a bag for a refillable water bottle and snacks. You will regret leaving your nourishment in the hands of a fair organiser. I find it so irritating to have to walk halfway across a fair – which are essentially Tudor mazes in disguise – to quench my thirst, only to get distracted as to where I was and what I was looking at.

Art fairs are widely considered to be economically important but culturally quite lacking. I don't think any art dealer, despite the huge sums they are forking out to display their artist's work, would argue that an art fair provides the best viewing conditions for art. The stands are uniform: usually plain white walls, plain flooring, and strong electric lighting, which all make for a lack of atmosphere. The general feeling is a temporary kind of manufactured plenitude. The late American artist John Baldessari got straight to the ick factor by comparing an artist visiting an art fair to a teenager barging into their parents' bedroom when they are having sex. I had the good fortune to meet Baldessari once, ironically at Art Basel Miami, and I asked him about this famous quote. He expanded it to say that for artists, trading art so openly is just like your parents sex life: You know it has to happen, but you just don't want to talk about it.

What art fairs lack in organic qualities or genuine creative flair they often make up for in collateral activities like parties, people-watching, and often accompanying 'art weeks'. Fairs are such a mainstay of the calendar that a whole art ecosystem is built around them, with museums opening key exhibitions to coincide, mainstream newspapers offering fair-related art features, and galleries putting on their most ambitious shows during the coveted art fair moment. Fairs have been great at stirring up new audiences and increased attention for contemporary art and now attract very large audiences. If you want to go next-level art addict and start regularly visiting art fairs, it could really pay off in the long run (for advice on how to improve your art fair experience, see page 225). I can't imagine my career without art fairs – the chance to see a truly global line-up, with many galleries flying in material specially, much of which is created exclusively for the fair (a kind of 'box-fresh' art). Fairs are a powerful snapshot of the current international art landscape. Even so, by the Sunday of a Frieze week, I'd rather put a fork in my eye than look at any more art.

ART BIENNIALS - IF A MUSEUM AND AN ART FAIR HAD A LOVE CHILD

Like art fairs, art biennials happen all over the world, are temporary, and bring together enormous amounts of largely contemporary art into one or multiple spaces. Unlike art fairs, biennials are not commercial endeavours, meaning nothing is for sale (but there are always art dealers lurking, who might eventually sell the work on display, albeit discreetly). Art fairs last a few days, whereas a biennial can last for a few months, with an opening preview that is usually attended by invited art-world figures: museum directors, curators, cultural leaders, and lots of glorious art-world eccentrics. They usually happen every two years (hence the name), with a different curator nominated to organise the selection. For artists, it is incredibly prestigious to have work selected for inclusion: participating in a biennial means that key art-world figures will see their work, which is likely to improve their career standing. John Baldessari (he was very quotable on the peccadillos of the art world) said that the art world was so status-obsessed that it would be simpler to offer a military-style uniform to artists, with stripes on the shoulder for every biennial presentation and a medal for a major museum retrospective. I agree that these kinds of events are like a school popularity contest and create something of a pressure cooker for those involved, whether as someone trying to be invited to great parties or an artist trying to get their work shown (though these can be the same people).

The first of its kind was the Venice Biennale, which was founded in 1895 and is still going strong as the world's largest art biennial. It's very much like the art-world Olympics, with pavilions for different countries and awards for the best presentation. No one would be caught dead in Lycra though, and the clothes are very much a consideration for those attending the preview, which has become a bit of a mini-fashion-show moment. The opening days are a spectacle of 'see and be seen', and even the most robust of egos can take a hammering in what feels like a permanent competition to be invited, attend events, meet famous art-world figures, discover an exciting exhibit, and stay sane on a diet of champagne and limited sleep. Although it is glitzy, and full of odd characters and people with dubious motives, I love witnessing the general bonhomie: it's charming to see how eager everyone is for the art, rushing around, desperate to get one more fix.

After the preview days, the public can visit the Venice Biennale by buying a pass. It is staged in multiple locations, but the highest density of art (where most of the national pavilions are housed) is in the Venice Giardini and neighbouring Arsenale. There are other pavilions across the city too, as well as official and non-official exhibitions. In the 2024 edition, which had the theme 'Foreigners Everywhere', there were a staggering number of pavilions and exhibitions, far too many for one person to be able to take in.

Although Venice is the most famous biennial, there are many others in cities such as Liverpool, São Paulo, and Sydney. Manifesta is a nomadic European biennial, and there's also Documenta in Kassel, Germany, which confusingly takes place every five years. I find art biennials are very exciting now that I have been attending them for a long time, but like art fairs, I would be lying if I said this was a gentle way to look at art. There is an abundance of work, and you have to make peace with the fact you will certainly miss brilliant things and waste time with displays that do nothing for you.

Finding works that do nothing for you will be true in all these places, though. Perhaps the greatest skill anyone looking at art gets to learn is how to believe that the *next* thing will be amazing, keeping the faith alive for what's around the corner. However, it is far easier to be open to what comes next if you have already given some thought to the age-old question: but is it art?

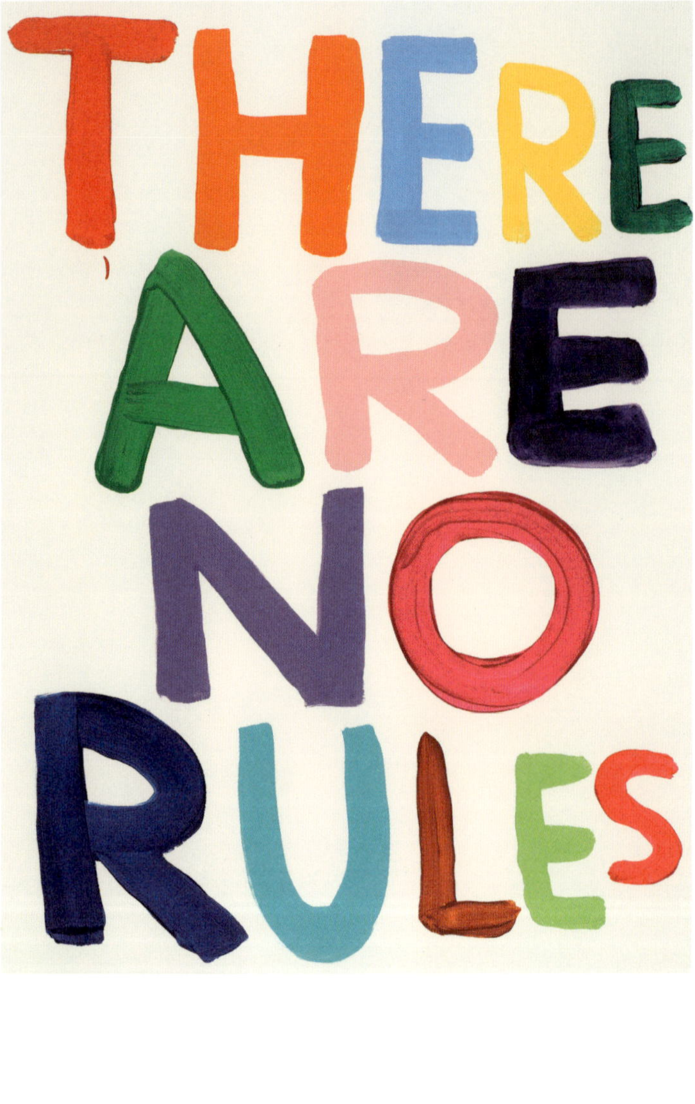
THERE
ARE
NO
RULES

WHAT IS ART?

So far, we've looked at where we can find art, but have not actually established what we're looking for. So, let's ask the all-important question: what is art?

The answer: anything can be art.

Yes, *anything*. That's why it's a bit confusing. Gone are the days when you trained like an art ninja to carve some marble or blend oil paints to faithfully represent something from the real world in a widely recognised and accepted artistic format. We live in a time when the carefully constructed narrative of what we might call 'traditional art' has been blown to smithereens. The fact is that, since the early twentieth century, absolutely anything can be 'art' – think of an unmade bed (Tracey Emin), a shark in formaldehyde (Damien Hirst), or an upturned urinal (Marcel Duchamp).

It's tempting to think it was all so much simpler back in those days of marble and oil paints, when we all knew what we were looking at and were mostly looking at the same kind of things over and over. Then, before we know it – and let's just for a moment crudely say that this all began when Picasso started jumbling up human faces – Andy Warhol's out there doing deadpan paintings of soup can labels. If we work on the basis for a second that our fundamental confusion about what art is in this society is Picasso's fault (and I love it when things are Picasso's fault, as he was a total prick to the women in his life but annoyingly also found time to be a creative revolutionary), then we need to consider for a moment *why* this art – modern art – has caused so much consternation for so long.

Art History – which is just history, but through the lens of art – is a relatively new discipline, and it was first written at the time when realism – showing a horse as a horse or a flower as a flower – reigned supreme. Art was supposed to represent *things*. It was that simple. But this type of art, touted and shaped by Western academics, lasted for just a fraction of the time (from about the early fifteenth century to the end of the nineteenth) we've been on this planet expressing ourselves. So, let's go back further in time, before the creation of art as a professional pursuit as we understand it today. Because by looking at art on a greater timespan, it becomes clear that it has been possible for *anything* to be art *since the dawn of humankind*. I want to show why this is a cause for celebration and something that can help us to grow our relationship with art. I'm not saying you need to know the rules to take part; I am saying there are no rules – which is a kind of freedom but perhaps one that feels a tad scary. I want to show how we might have become victims of a long, slow cultural obfuscation whereby we've become convinced that not only is there a right and wrong way to approach art but also that there's a right way and a wrong way to *make* art.

And if you don't have a position on what counts as art, as well as a good grounding in when it historically came into existence, it can be hard to feel confident in engaging with a piece of art or an artist.

So, let's take a moment to skip through a ludicrously brief consideration of what has constituted art throughout time.

Art-wise, *Homo sapiens* (that's us) started out with cave painting some 40,000 years ago. Many examples of cave painting are what we could call representational – in that they represent something we find in the observable world, such as wild animals. There are also a lot of handprints (which are still going strong in children's nurseries the world over), as well as abstract cave paintings, in which any specific *thing* can't be readily identified, so they might well be non-referential, simply offering visual or emotional stimuli. Little is known about the creators of these works, but let's face it, it's highly unlikely that all these paintings were created by 'artists' in the sense that we would understand that term today. No one was sporting a beret in their rock studio. In fact, there is some suggestion that a lot of these paintings were created by women, but for what purpose, and in what context, we do not know.*

*Hughes, V. (2013), 'Were the first artists mostly women?' *National Geographic,* www.nationalgeographic.com/adventure/article/131008-women-handprints-oldest-neolithic-cave-art

Although cave art is clearly a form of creative expression and had a decorative function, it is also thought that it could have served ritualistic purposes tied to the rhythms and aspirations of life – for instance, conjuring bison on the wall before going out to hunt for them.[*] I am not trying to romanticise things, since our earliest ancestors spent most of their time trying not to starve and/or be eaten by lions, but art was an inseparable part of being alive. The art left in sites all over the world is how our earliest human ancestors communicate with us in the present day, a thought that gives me goosebumps. In this context, art is a form of communication, a form of ritual and of beauty. There's even a theory that people would travel large distances, risking their lives to obtain rare pigments with which to paint.[†]

As we move beyond the hunter-gatherer period, vast civilisations were formed on all continents that had humans knocking around on them in what is known as ancient history, which refers to the period from 3,000 BCE to 500 CE.[‡] In the ancient world, humans began to leave behind ever more impressive cultural records. Art was a central aspect of life, a way of

---

[*] Clottes, J., Lewis-Williams, D. (1998), *The Shamans of Prehistory: Trance and Magic in the Painted Caves*, New York, NY: Harry N Abrams.

[†] 'Prehistory', Pigments Through the Ages, www.webexhibits.org/pigments/intro/early. html/

[‡] 'BCE' and 'CE' stand for 'before the common era' and 'common era', respectively. Also known as BC and AD.

expressing religion, power, and riches, and led to some staggering feats of creative ingenuity from ancient civilisations like the Mesopotamians in the Middle East, the Aztecs and Incas in Latin America, and the Greco-Roman world. We can marvel at the profound vision of artistic achievements that have been discovered, such as the Terracotta Warriors, which were begun in China in 246 BC, or the tomb of King Tutankhamun, which was created in Egypt over 3,300 years ago.

Neither of these works is the vision of a single artist, nor were they created solely as art: they served a specific purpose as funerary monuments and invaluable objects for the afterlife. In fact, there are very few ancient artists whose names we know and to whom we can accurately ascribe work. Historians search hard for them in the small amount of written evidence that remains of this time, because we are so accustomed to the idea of a named and greatly talented individual – an idea that was born in the next period we will jump to, the Renaissance, which is often regarded as the high point of Western art history and took place between the fourteenth and seventeenth centuries.

The Renaissance didn't happen overnight. It followed on from the medieval period, which emerged in Europe around 500 CE. This was a period defined by Christianity establishing itself in Europe (with some challenge from Islam in parts of Spain) and the battle for territory that had previously been part of the Roman Empire. For roughly 1,000 years, building churches and filling them with devotional art that offered a narrative illustration of the Bible (a new book and an instant bestseller!) was the name of the game. Western medieval art was decidedly functional: it gave instruction to the congregation, almost of all whom would have been illiterate.

But things get a bit spicier art-wise in the Renaissance. Although there were professional artist studios in the medieval period, and many artists of renown, it's in the Renaissance that we start to really see the cult of the individual genius. Think of rivals like Raphael and Michelangelo and lauded masterminds like Leonardo, who was so in demand he worked for foreign powers. The Renaissance is synonymous with Italy, but it was happening across Europe, and it was during this time that the quest for realism went through the roof. It was the duty of art, still tied to worship, to emulate and imitate God's creations: to capture all living things, but especially human bodies, the natural world, and architecture in a way that made the things depicted seem *real*.

Renaissance artists considered themselves part of a thrilling forward push, of an age of progress and rapid development. The Renaissance was a rebirth, a flowering of the arts that looked to the future but also harnessed the past. Critical to its development was a new appreciation and respect for the ancient cultures of Greece and Rome, which is why mythological figures from a distant pagan world were reintroduced as subjects – sculptures of Hercules, or paintings of Venus. Despite these new non-Christian subjects (which added major titillation to paintings, as artists could get away with depicting Venus, the goddess of love, wearing far fewer clothes than the Virgin Mary), the themes of Renaissance art were completely tied to power, religion, and status. This was the first time that artists were courted and paid huge sums – in today's money, Michelangelo would have been a millionaire. But Renaissance artists didn't enjoy autonomy: they were always working in the service of great powers like popes, kings, and dukes, who dictated what was made, where it was displayed, and who got to see it. There were no museums, auction houses, or solo exhibitions, and no discipline of Art History (although from the mid-sixteenth century we do have the first biographies of artists, written by a chap called Vasari).

After the Renaissance, Western art became even more codified during the Enlightenment in the seventeenth and eighteenth centuries. Art doesn't get much more conventional than it was in this era. It might have been a period of scientific discovery, but art was still tied to power – artists couldn't go it alone without great patrons – and realism still reigned supreme. The

Enlightenment was an era of refinement, when notions of 'great' art and 'high culture' were polished, categorised, and shaped. Ideas of what is – and isn't – art were formalised by the building of museums with great collections, much of which was obtained through colonial plundering. It was also the time when art education became structured, with the creation of institutes such as the Royal Academy in London, the Académie des Beaux-Arts in Paris, and the various Accademie di Belle Arti across Italy.

In the Enlightenment, treatises were written that defined a pecking order in terms of subject matter: historical paintings glorifying wars were deemed far worthier than poor old floral still lifes – a subject deemed suitable for 'lady painters'. In other unsavoury ways, a ranking in terms of global status began to emerge and – funnily enough, for something written by European men – everything made in the West, like Greco-Roman art and Renaissance paintings, was at the top, with anything made in non-European locations deemed 'primitive'. Sculptures, paintings, and architectural wonders were designated as the highest art forms. Many other mediums that have existed worldwide for thousands of years – weaving and other textile arts, pottery, bead work, wood work – were excluded from the category of 'art' and demoted to being 'crafts', with an inbuilt value-judgement that deemed them lacking in intellectual properties and made solely for appearance without any invention.

These categorisations, which still organise much mainstream art and underpin a lot of education today, were incredibly Eurocentric, which means that they leave out vast swathes of rich artistic creativity. However, today there are lots of places to find an expanded sense of art history, such as *The Infinite Image* by Zainab Bahrani and *The History of Art: A Global View* by Jean Robertson and Deborah Hutton, who, alongside other expert authors, chart a refreshingly global narrative.

Following this period of intense classification came the industrial age, which takes us through the nineteenth century and into the world we know today. The industrial age was a major moment for our purposes here because it marks, in many imaginations, the break between the art of the past and the art of 'now', a phrasing that suggests a major art civil war – which, in a way, there was.

The industrial age was a time of economic boom, with cities developing at a staggering rate and the birth of extraordinary inventions, such as the steam engine, electric lights, and the camera. The camera had a seismic effect on art: what were artists to do in the face of something that literally represented the world through a lens – and quickly, too? Wasn't that art's job?

In addition to these upending inventions, Western society started to become less strictly divided between the haves (royalty, aristocrats, landed gentry – the moneybags) and the have nots (servants, paupers, workers – the commoners), with a growing group of 'have some things, get more things' – better known as the middle classes. These guys were new money: they enjoyed leisure time when they were not working, and they started to buy art to furnish their homes. The middle classes were instrumental in artists having modes of showing and selling work that didn't rely on the patronage of a small group of people. This new market would lead to the solo show and the artist as an independent person painting what they liked, embodied perfectly by the group of artists who bridge the gap between the end of the industrial age and the birth of modern art: the Impressionists.

Today, Impressionism is a beloved art movement, easy to fall for and easy on the eye, which means that it's not cool to say you love it (though I do really love Monet, the painter of all those water lilies). But back in the 1870s and 1880s, the age in which these artists were working, they were seen as strange interlopers, disrupting traditional principles of realism and the agreed order of things. They were modern artists, and they painted a modern world. Gone were portraits of the landed gentry hunting, and in came pictures of working-class people drinking, middle-class people catching trains, and leisured people enjoying theatre shows where women revealed their undergarments (think the Moulin Rouge). To top it off, they painted all this in a loose style that broke all the rules surrounding formal composition, idealised subject matter, traditional perspectives, focused scenes with neat lines, and the moderate use of colour – all of which were being rigorously taught at the art academies of the time. I find it instructive and even comforting to know that Impressionism, one of the major stepping stones to today's contemporary art, was ridiculed in its day and is now so popular as to be a bit embarrassing to trendy art-world people.

We are now entering the period of the much-fabled modern art – a term that can be used to cover a ridiculously broad period of history, from around the advent of Impressionism in 1860 to 1970. But arguably the most ground-breaking and truly 'modern' work happened at the turn of the twentieth century. By then, Europe was enjoying democracy (of sorts, as long as you weren't poor or, heaven forbid, a woman). The role of the church had gradually lessened, and philosophers like Nietzsche were coming to grips with how our values should look in a world without God. In the modern age, when art was no longer solely made for powerful religious and political structures, the big question was: what was art for now?

Modern artists became synonymous with a new order of disorder. Modern art was about new art for new audiences, for new reasons, and in new ways. Artists no longer wanted to be chained to realism, to hide their feelings for the greater good of academic art, to deny their artistic impulses and flights of fancy. The birth of psychology helped society to wrestle with the nature of existence, and modern artists poured this into their work. Artists became central figures and not just service providers. They existed in increasing numbers, showed in their own exhibitions, and created their own organised movements like Futurism, complete with their own manifestos. Art hopped along from one 'ism' to the next, with artists arguing about what the true purpose of art was. Art had never been so self-conscious.

The emergence of modern art was like a Pandora's box: rules that had been set down were bent every which way. But I'd say the biggest grenade was thrown by French artist Marcel Duchamp. Duchamp was the ultimate art-world disruptor, because he presented a radical concept. He said that anything can be art if the artist says it is art. *Fountain*, his most famous work, dating from 1917, was a ready-made object – a 'found' urinal that he signed and turned on its side. Duchamp was largely seen as a joker at the time, but his endeavour was serious and had profound consequences. Today, most artists owe a debt to the liberation offered by Duchamp. He allowed art to be playful, experimental, and philosophical all at the same time, and his influence meant that artists could approach big ideas in a myriad of ways that were not previously imaginable. This did not happen immediately. In the intervening decades, Surrealism and abstract art would come to be the leading trends of modern art. It was not until the 1960s that Duchamp's ideas were fully explored and revived, when Pop artists like Warhol came along and used 'found' imagery by recreating mass-produced objects like Brillo boxes and Campbell's soup cans. Pop Art, roughly speaking, marked the end of modern art, a period when what art was made of, how it was made (or not made at all), what it stood for, and what it meant were all up for grabs.

Now, around 1970, we come to contemporary art. A quick aside about terminology before we begin: contemporary art is a tricky term because it means 'RIGHT NOW' but it also means 'FIFTY YEARS AGO'. It also suggests that the artists under discussion are living – and yet there are plenty of artists who were working in the 1980s who are now no longer with us. Can they be contemporary artists and dead at the same time? Also, it's true to say that Leonardo was a *contemporary* of Michelangelo and also that they were both, technically speaking, *contemporary* artists in their day. (I don't make the rules, but if I were Queen of Art History for a day – and I'd love the outfit – I would insist that we rename these most recent and current time periods for clarity, as it's a total nightmare.)

Regardless of unhelpful terminology, it's safe to say that the legacy of modern art today in our contemporary art moment is a booming creative landscape replete with many modes of art-making: abstract art, conceptual art, found art, site-specific art, experiential art, installation art, and much more (for more handy genre tips, see the glossary on page 307).

WHAT IS ART NOW?

A major problem is that we have been so busy creating a linear story of art history that goes from A to B that we have made things sit in opposition to one another instead of in tandem. It's pitched as a battle between the old stuff and the new stuff, which creates unnecessary tension.

To argue that realistic art is either better or worse than what follows is to make an error, because it suggests that people have to make a choice between thinking either that more contemporary-looking art forms are a wrong turn, or that they represent progress and render more traditional forms obsolete. But it doesn't have to be a choice, and of course traditional forms *are* contemporary, in the sense that there are lots of amazing artists working right now still using those techniques.

However, the predominant belief that the *point* of art is to be realistic has taken such strong hold that it still threatens to make all other art 'lesser'. It is easy to see this play out in our own lives. As small children we start making art with complete freedom, but then we start to associate something looking technically accomplished as being 'better'. We are moulded to make art 'correct' – as in more realistic – and maybe also start to learn about famous artworks like Leonardo's *Mona Lisa*. As a result, what becomes ingrained is a reverence for the tradition of realism. This kind of belief also pressures audiences who have been told there are rules to follow in art, and that there is an order to everything that must be studied and obeyed. The forcefulness of this traditional narrative started to imprison us.

Modern art offered a kind of freedom. Arguably, it returned art to a purer state, one less governed by rules. One that allowed artists to be at the centre of their creations, expressing themselves directly to their audience without the intermediary of an academy, a church, or those who held power. The American philosopher Arthur Danto talks about 'the end of art' – meaning no more rules, not no more pictures. He writes that what we in the West have traditionally called 'Art' (with a capital A) is very much the result of a specific kind of historical process – a process that, as we have seen, was first aimed at representing things exactly, and then, when that broke down, at interrogating exactly what art was, leading to the age of the manifesto and the movement. But that process came to an end via Duchamp and later via people like Warhol – artists who help us remember that what makes something a work of art isn't always anything specific about its material. Instead, *anything* can be art. Art is freed from trying to represent, and freed from interrogating itself – it can just be art again. Art is about embodying meaning: about giving us a place to sense-make, and to make sense of the world. We see this at work in the paintings of the Old Masters as much as in those of the Cubists and Abstract Impressionists. So, rather than making us choose one way over another, we are now freed to enjoy it all.

I like these sentiments; they mean we can step away from the classifications and hierarchy of art history. For a long time, the unwritten rule was that the public had to educate themselves about art to be allowed in the room (I believed this and so I did it). But now I think it has to be the other way around: the art world needs to educate itself about its audiences, as all people have the ability to commune with and experience art. We can engage with art in a similar fashion to how we all engage with music – in different ways and with different knowledge and musical abilities, as we always have. Some art you might study in a book, some you might want to see on a special trip to an exhibition, some you might make at home with your friends and family, some is more refined and appreciated and some less so, but all of it is art.

We are standing in the aftermath of a 500-year period when Western art was corseted, wound up tightly, and made to stand to attention. There are cultures all over the world that have never institutionalised and categorised their art-making. I can't quite believe that our ancestors were so hung up over the question, 'What is art?' Now we too can breathe more deeply and reconnect with our natural instincts towards art and art-making. So, to conclude, not only is the temple of art wide open for you to enter exactly as you are, but you can also build it however you like.

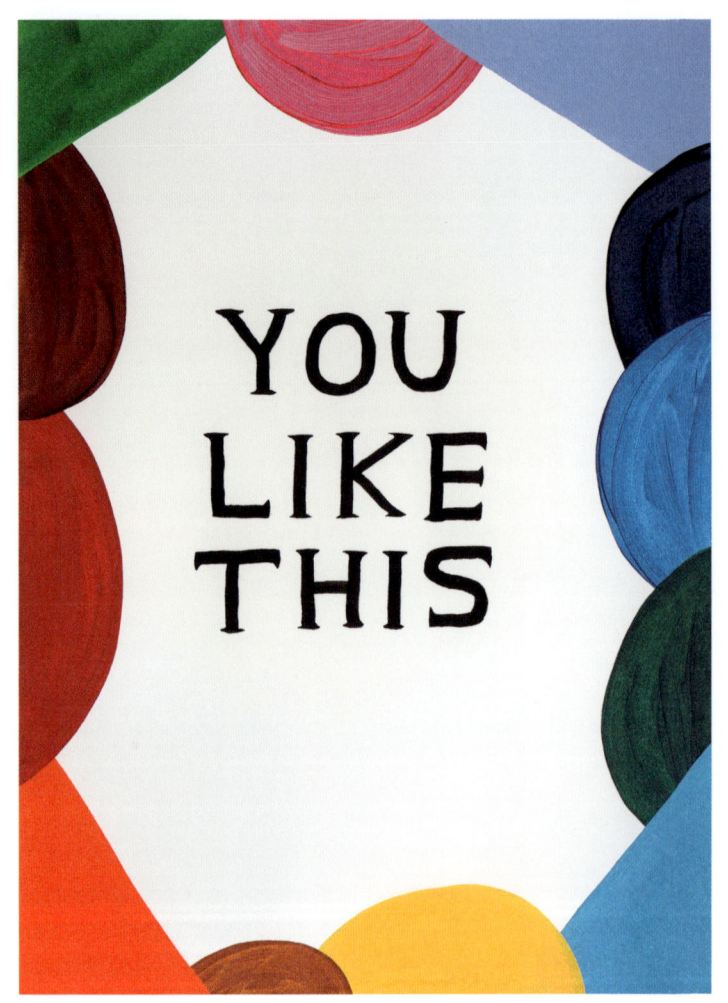

PART TWO :
WHAT TO DO WHEN
YOU'RE IN FRONT
OF AN ARTWORK

How to Speak About Art You Like

I used to run contemporary art galleries, first in Hong Kong and then in London. Between the ages of twenty-six and thirty-six, I was an art dealer, meaning I sold art made by living artists, which came straight from their studios for exhibitions in the gallery. I helped to birth the art into the world, and I spoke about it with clients and people who popped in to see what was showing.

You might assume that, when I began, I was somehow qualified to do this having completed, by that point, *two* degrees in Art History. You'd be wrong. I knew how to talk and write about the art of the past; I could wang on about Michelangelo for days because I could follow texts and theory that had been cultivated for hundreds of years. But when it came to unwrapping an artwork by a young painter that no one else had seen before, I was vulnerable – it was all so exposed and raw. Often there was no text, no guidelines for this artist or this body of work. I was part of making its story and helping it to find its place in the world. I was simultaneously ter-rified and thrilled by this prospect, and stayed working in contemporary art for this reason.

I had to learn quickly that my role was to give a voice to the art, to help it reach its audience by understanding the artist's process, background, and motivations. Unlike when I was working on a Michelangelo exhibition in my first job at the British Museum, I had the living artist with me to get to know and plenty of freshly made work to study, and I used the information I was gathering in real time to put on exhibitions. I learned how to make the art look its best by curating the pieces, which involved arranging them in a certain order so that they worked well together and separately. What would look best in the window? What could survive that slightly darker corner over there? Would the whole show benefit from painting the walls a darker colour, to produce more contrast? Where was the least intrusive place to put the labels? Which artwork would make a great image to promote the show?

I also wrote the press release for each show and created a language around the works. Some artists are incredibly articulate and can manage this themselves, but most of them tend to make art to express the things they find hard to say. I have often heard someone innocently ask an artist, 'What do you think about X?', in response to which the tongue-tied artist will simply point to the artwork on display and say something like, 'Everything I think is in the work.' The American painter Georgia O'Keeffe put this beautifully: 'I found I could say things with colour and shapes that I couldn't say any other way – things I had no words for.'

I realised there was value to be found in acting as a bridge between the artist, their work, and the viewer. And, as a dealer, that value could well turn out to be financial: if I could help the viewer along, they would hopefully buy an artwork and therefore turn into a client who supported the artist's practice. I frequently found that although people could tell me which artworks they loved, perhaps even enough to buy them, they struggled to articulate why, and not being able to do so made them distrust the sensation or not value their innate response as they ought to.

It's a fairly common occurrence for people to clam up in front of an artwork. Not only are we scared to get it 'wrong', but also we can struggle to verbalise the strong emotions that art may stir. By spending more time with art, these sensations can be allowed more time and space to get heard, and we can try to tune in to the particular way a work makes us feel. It may never have occurred to you that art can change your entire mood, but it can. Bring to mind a work of art that makes you smile – or even better, go visit it or look at it online while thinking about the effect it has on you. What is it that you are feeling? When art makes you feel good, it does so in such a way as to infiltrate your soul, a place where language doesn't easily reach.

Just as with music or food that hits the spot, it is often very difficult to articulate the exact feeling that art gives you and why exactly it is happening. It might relate to something from your childhood, or remind you of someone or something you love. Picasso is absurdly quotable, and this is one of his best which relates so well to the powerful relationship between art objects and the human psyche: 'Art is a lie that makes us realise truth.' Art you love cuts through; it *connects* like it was always part of you and you have only just noticed it there. Great art can communicate through centuries, time, and space – it is, after all, the physical remnant of a human, alive or dead, who you will probably never meet, telling you something about how they see the world.

Here are some ways to help you break down and think about what that connection means. I am not being scientific or mathematical about loving art (as if I have ever been mathematical about anything, even math). After all, very few of us break down every chord penned by the Beatles to understand why we like their songs so much; perhaps we feel that to do so might take away from the energising experience of their creations. But I want to help you *own* your emotions and responses to art. That was my role at the gallery. I would see people light up in front of something and had to tread a fine line between over-explaining the magic of the work (sometimes if you know how the trick is performed it loses its power) and lending the viewer a vocabulary that was useful in verbally articulating their feelings.

Let's go back to the Beatles for a moment. 'Penny Lane' is a universally loved song, but it would be wrong to think we are all experiencing the same emotion when we hear it. My dad heard this song released in real time, so for him it would have sounded completely new and original. Then my dad played it to me as a child in the 1980s, so I have a whole other layer of nostalgia attached to it – the same piece of music operates on two different time scales within one family. The same is true for art. Take one of my favourite pictures as a child, *Marilyn Diptych* by Andy Warhol. Warhol 'appropriated' (art-world speak for 'stole') a black and white press image for a Marilyn Monroe movie. He transformed it into a silkscreen and amped up the colours so her hair is banana yellow, her face is bubble-gum pink, her lips are cherry red, and her collar is turquoise. The colourful image of Marilyn repeats twenty-five times, in five rows of five rows. Sitting adjacent to the twenty-five colourful Marilyns are twenty-five tiles of black and white Marilyn, but they are imperfect, like when your printer does its best to spurt out your pages when it is running out of ink.

There are people alive today who saw this as a freshly produced image in New York in 1962, an attention-grabbing work of Pop Art. Maybe they worked in advertising or film, which might have added another layer of personal connection to the work. I can't ever have that experience. I will always see it through the lens of my own history, as a British woman who grew up as part of a generation in the 1980s and 1990s that was taught to idolise everything American. Furthermore, I saw the artwork as a child in a book, and I didn't have any context for it – I just knew I loved it.

Let me try to explain why without any art historical chat, since at the time 'pop' to me was the fizzy drink we only saw in the pantry at Christmas (my mum was a dental nurse). But I didn't need any knowledge of Pop Art to ground my desire. I knew I wanted to keep finding that page with that picture again and again. Why? I loved the colour, those inorganic, unnatural, bold tones. I loved the brazen quality of it. Marilyn didn't look like a beautiful woman in a magazine any more – she looked like a superhero. I loved the smudgy lines, how it was imperfect. It managed to be two things at once: a mass media image and a hand-made artwork. It screamed 'AMERICA' to me. It screamed 'POWERFUL WOMAN'. Now, as an adult woman aware of Monroe's demise and her appalling treatment by men and the media, I can't see it quite in the same way. But Warhol chose something that connected to me, and showed it to me in such a fashion that it cut through and therefore evolves with me as I evolve. I will play my daughter the Beatles, and she will add more layers to the family's listening. I will show her *Marilyn Diptych*, and she'll have her own distinct set of takeaways (I was only one generation removed from Pop Art – yeesh, I am old – but 1962 to her may as well be 1862).

I am aware I am talking about the very obscure talents that are the Beatles and Andy Warhol. No one is getting a gold medal for pointing out that they are loveable – they're the very definition of pop (as in popular) art. At the small galleries I worked at, I didn't come close to an Andy Warhol. I had to help to find these touch points with completely new talent. I needed to identify what happened in the nebulous journey between the artist's mind and their reception beyond the studio. When I began working in galleries, I was like a contemporary art midwife: I didn't make the work but, with the artist's support, I could be instrumental in bringing new pieces into the world. What follows are the questions I had to ask, and which I hope you might find useful when learning to 'read' works of art.

I ENJOYED LOOKING AT THE RED PAINTING

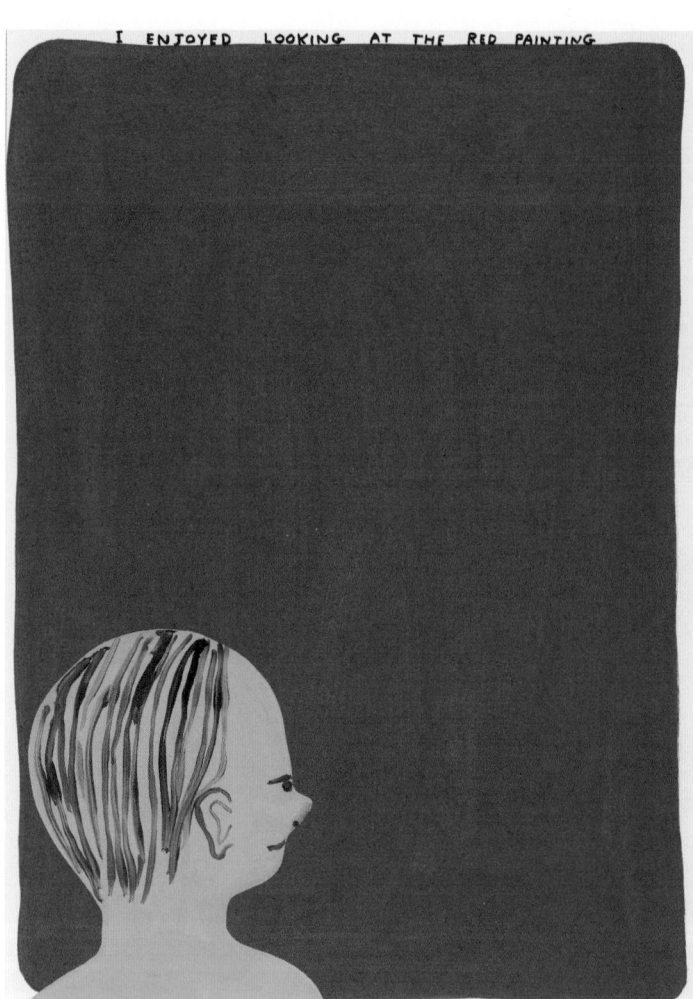

HOW TO READ
AN ARTWORK

HOW DID THEY MAKE IT ?

This is the most objective place to start: what is the piece made of? As much as I think art can be pure magic and so precious as to be completely priceless, I have to pull back the *Wizard of Oz* curtain and emphasise that it's all just human-made *stuff*. Even Rembrandt's alarmingly lifelike portraits are simply canvas and oil paint. Rodin's *The Kiss* might make your heart ache, but it's technically a block of cut marble.

Every gallery will make sure you know what the exhibited art is made of, but that's just the beginning. Very rarely do we marvel *only* at the medium (i.e. what it's made of). The materials are usually a means to an end. Of course, this being art, there are always exceptions to the rule, particularly from the twentieth century, when there were art movements that drew attention to the materials themselves in a purposefully self-conscious way. My favourite of these is a movement originating in Italy, Arte Povera, which was all about 'poor materials' such as lowly wood scraps and even soil, rags, and twigs. Even then though, there was a profound message behind the work: the artists of the movement wanted to question long-accepted notions of value and status (marble is expensive; artworks made in it are valuable) and instead to elevate humble materials. They were particularly keen to do this at a time when rapid industri-alisation in Italy threatened an older way of life.

Even when there are almost no materials, as with artists who take a 'concept-first' approach and reject the need to physically 'craft' anything – meaning it's more about the idea of the artwork than perhaps what it looks and feels like – it is possible for the work to have an abundance of meaning. Think of someone like Yves Klein, famous for creating and patenting his own colour, International Klein Blue, who once staged an exhibition in Paris that I wish I could have 'seen'. Around 3,000 people heard about it, formed a queue, and entered to discover he had emptied the gallery except for an empty cabinet, painted it white, and added a blue arrival curtain. He would have described his 'medium' as the void he created: the absence of materi-als was the point. You don't have to agree with his message (I think it was a slice of genius that pointed out cultural expectations and art-world hierarchies while dismissing the idea of the artist as physical 'maker' and amplifying them as 'thinkers'), but you can perhaps see that the medium was in some sense there but, again, not enough on its own.

WHAT IS THE TECHNIQUE ?

The next question you might want to ask is: *how* was it made? What is the technique? Paint is the most common medium in art, but style and technique take it in divergent directions – Picassos and Rembrandts look completely different, though both artists were broadly using the exact same stuff. There are lots of different types of paint and artists have been demonstrating the versatility of them for hundreds of years. Indeed, Cecily Brown, a much-coveted British artist working today, talks about confronting the weighty history of paint: 'The boundaries of painting excite me. You've got the same old materials – just oils and a canvas – and you're trying to do something that's been done for centuries.'

Technique is how an artist wields their material; it's the way to have a particular style. For instance, someone like the American Abstract Expressionist Jackson Pollock was splashing paint all over the place, whereas 300 years earlier Vermeer was using microscopic brushes to paint thin layers with the precise care of someone trying to defuse a bomb. A general rule of thumb is that the greater the originality of an artist's technique, the more distinct their style. Rembrandt not only created thick paint passages called impasto, but also combined them with sheer layers of thin paint known as glaze to create a luminous effect. By pushing and pulling between these thin and thick paint applications, he could achieve unparalleled results. Picasso, on the other hand, used paint in a blunter way, using a palette knife (a paint-mixing knife) to make rough marks. He was also one of the first artists to use ordinary house paint in some of his works, possibly because it gave a glossier finish.

When you are looking at a painting, think about *how* the paint has gone down on the canvas or board. Can you see the marks of the brushes? Does the paint look wild and abandoned or controlled and tightly handled?

Is there lots of it or not much of it? Is the surface cracked with age? Can you see how the artist has adapted the work as they went along, such as overpainting or leaving just exposed bare canvas untouched by paint? When I am confronted with a painting I know nothing about, sometimes this simple act of focusing on just the paint application is enough to satisfy me, and often generates feelings and thoughts about the piece.

If you are looking at a sculpture, materials are important to identify and understand, but beyond that, think about how a sculpture occupies space. Is it a traditional bust – head and shoulders on a plinth – installed at head height so you can 'converse' with the subject? Is it made from 'found' materials, which means things that had a life before they entered an artist's studio? (Found materials can be literally *anything*, from bicycle wheels – like Ai Weiwei and Marcel Duchamp – to bottle tops, like the artist El Anatsui, who makes beautiful modern tapestries with them by flattening and weaving the metal strips.) Is it something that feels human in scale or something that dwarfs the viewer and commands all the energy in the room? Do you like some of the sculptures more than others? Is it the same type that you like each time? If it is, what's different about the ones you do and don't like? This might be to do with style.

WHAT IS THE STYLE?

This goes back to what I was saying earlier about the *way* an artist has used the material. Though Picasso and

Rembrandt both used paint and brushes, their techniques were very different. Even more so, their objectives varied, and the combination of these factors gave rise to different styles. One of Picasso's many styles became known as cubism (developed with his friend, the artist Georges Braque, around 1907), so called because he reduced the picture to lots of small square shapes in his pursuit of revolutionising the way that reality was translated by the artist. His paint was used in the service of a style that 'undid' reality and started to break up the picture. On the other hand, Rembrandt was a Baroque artist (a style that dominated seventeenth-century European art), who prioritised drama and emotion by using paint in such a way that his subjects felt real to the viewer.

Sometimes an artist has a style all of their own, but often they're working in a way that is shared by other artists. Just like how there are fashions in clothing or written styles in books, art has fashions too. One of the most commonly known styles is Impressionism, which is all about loose brushwork, giving an impression of a scene, person, or object, rather than presenting it 'realistically' by copying it. Styles and 'isms' are not rigid borders though: you don't have to be a famous member of the Impressionist group (and it was indeed a formal exhibiting group for a while) like Monet to employ an Impressionistic style. You can also describe an artist as being Impressionistic, even if they died hundreds of years before Monet and the French movement of the nineteenth century. The late works of Rembrandt, Titian, and Tintoretto – by which I mean the works made at the end of their careers – are all great examples of Impressionism way before its time, and you could argue that some of David Hockney's work is Impressionistic even though he graduated from art school nearly a century after the first Impressionist exhibition.

WHAT DOES THE ARTWORK SAY TO YOU?

When thinking about what the artist is saying in the artwork, the real thing to consider is what are *you* seeing and getting from the artwork? The British artist Bridget Riley – still working in her nineties and famed for her bold 'op art' paintings – insists that her 'work is completed by the viewer'. Duchamp said much the same thing: 'A work of art exists only when the spectator has looked at it.' As much as a different kind of artist might wish to impart a clear, vivid message, they have to accept that, hundreds of years later, or even just days after they make it, an artwork will be in the world unchaperoned, and will become a vessel for new meanings and ideas.

I remember experiencing a breakthrough moment in my own journey as an art historian. In the first year of university, I submitted an essay on Victorian architecture (a subject which I found pretty dull) and permitted myself a little flight of fancy, in which I compared an overbearing, rigid architecture style with a totally unrelated painting that also made me feel the same kind of oppression. The tutor only left me one comment in the margin, which was to say that this was a novel idea and she enjoyed it. I has been so busy studying and trying to get everything 'right' that I hadn't yet noticed that my own opinions and thoughts were a valid part of the story.

We are individuals and therefore the effect that art has upon us can never be universal. Museums add labels to the wall to help us along, to give us some context, but don't think of them as the answer to the mystery of the picture. By all means, use them to aid your looking, but to stir you imagination the artwork itself is the best place to put your attention. Be specific in your looking, in the sense that you should put yourself and everything that makes you *you* in the centre of the activity. If van Gogh's *Sunflowers* make you feel lonely when everyone else is saying they make them feel joyful, then don't dampen that thought – nurture it. Just because something's been repeated a lot in books doesn't mean it's the only valid response to a work of art.

Indeed, artists can help us with this: they have to trust their own instincts all the time to create what they care about. We too must trust our instincts as viewers of art. Try to resist the pressure to conform to an accepted version of things. The more time you spend looking at – and talking about – art, the easier and more natural this will feel. There is so much to discover when it comes to appreciating art – you could study for a lifetime – but I have always found that the four questions discussed in this chapter are plenty to consider for any new piece you encounter.

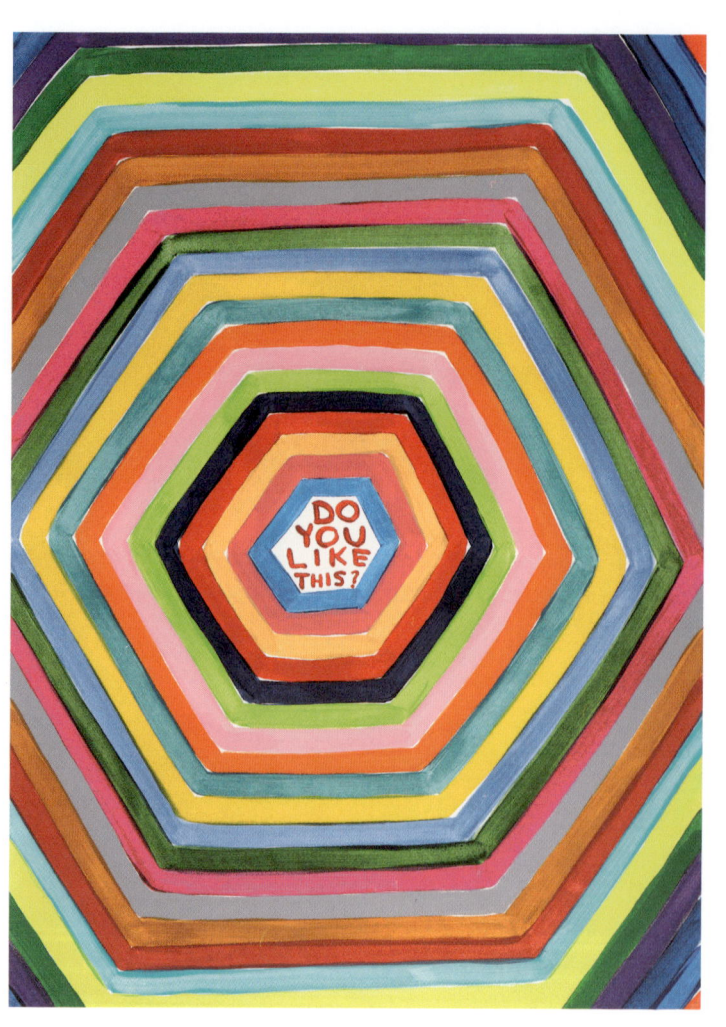

HOW TO SPEAK ABOUT ART YOU DO NOT LIKE

Just because anything can be art doesn't mean that all art has to be liked, appreciated, or enjoyed. I am not here to make you like everything. In fact, it's closer to the opposite: we should give ourselves permission to actively dislike things. You do it with music, you do it with movies, and you do it with books – now it's time to do it with art. I'm happy to share number one on my ick list, a chap from the past, an eighteenth-century Venetian painter called Canaletto, who just would not stop painting pictures of his hometown. There are loads of his scenes of canals in British museums. I dislike them all.

I also feel similarly about another Italian (otherwise I think Italian culture is damn near perfect), this time a sculptor called Antonio Canova, who was working in the whitest of white marble roughly around the same time, and who I believe was successful in creating things that say nothing at all. You can find his snooze-inducing artworks in museums across Italy and in most major world museums like the Met in New York and the Louvre in Paris.

Now that I have irritated any Canaletto and Canova fans, we should think about ways to articulate *why* we don't enjoy something. This is a great skill to have, and it's an important step in honing your thoughts and responses to art (which may change over time, of course, but as yet no development for me on the Canaletto front). I am not trying to make anyone else join my camp (except sometimes my husband when he gets excited by a Canova sculpture just to get on my nerves). But your responses to art mean something, so take them and use them to better equip yourself to see and experience more art, including building confidence in your legitimate opinions. Doing so will help you to reach a place where you can respect and appreciate a work of art without loving it or even really liking it. If you are not enjoying something, these notes might help point you in the direction of *why* not.

DOES IT LEAVE YOU FEELING COLD?

It is all very well and good to marvel at technical skill, but what about how it makes you feel? It might be useful to remember this analogy: a baker knows that a cake can be a splendid physical creation, but if it doesn't taste great it was all for nothing. For me this is the issue with Canova. His marble works are so refined, so polished, that they lack gusto. In their quest for perfection, they remove any emotional hooks. His work is not a million miles away from that of Gian Lorenzo Bernini, another Italian sculptor working in marble 150 years before Canova (he made most of his mega-hits between 1620 and 1650). For me, Bernini imbued his work with much greater expression than Canova. They are both theatrical artists, but where Canova tries so hard to be monumental and striking, Bernini is more subtle and ambiguous, not revealing everything at once. Canova leaves me unmoved and at a distance, while Bernini invites me to look closer.

A lot of people find public works of art to be quite cold, to the point that many of us simply call any bloke on a plinth a statue rather than a sculpture – the former being more a static symbol than a work of art – and don't think of them as works of art at all. It has come to much wider attention in recent years across the world that a lot of public art historically was designed to promote a strident message about power and continuity, and therefore expression or individuality are usually lacking. Furthermore, many of the subjects when seen in today's light no longer seem worth celebrating, what with their being beneficiaries of the enslavement of humans. So, if you feel you are lacking because the public art you encounter leaves you cold, I think it probably just means you are normal.

IS IT BORING?

Maybe there is not much going on. Maybe it's an abstract black and white painting. For some cool customers, this is just their bag, but for you it's fine to say, 'It's too minimalist to turn me on.'

Or maybe it's a bloke who repeatedly paints Venetian canals with these little people who feel like bad actors in a dull play. Why I am so frustrated by Canaletto? I think it's because Canaletto and the off-brand imitators who came after him are *everywhere* in British museums. They are so insistent in their presence and yet I find them to be empty promises. I lived in Venice for a while when I was at university, and later returned as an Art History tutor for short spells in my early twenties (which was as wonderful as it sounds). After spending so much time there, I've always felt Canaletto's paintings came up short. I was almost angry at them for failing to give me what I wanted – I expected them to transmit the kind of magnificence I felt when I was there, and they couldn't come close. To me they are like the Venetian-themed hotel I visited in Macau, China (think a gaudy twenty-first-century theme park for adults): everyone else thought it was a funny, charming parody, but I felt bitterly frustrated, like being reminded of a loved one I dearly missed and ached to touch again. I told Grayson Perry, a brilliant contemporary artist famed for his pottery and investigations into the British class system, how I felt about Canaletto, and braced myself for a telling off. But he surprised me by telling me he agreed completely, labelling it 'airless tourist art'.

Canaletto's paintings speak of an age when mega-posh people, who became known as Grand Tourists, went off on their privileged jollies around 'the Continent' and brought one back to hang like a big fat postcard above their fireplace. *'The Doge's Palace? Oh yes, you really must see it before you die, Tabitha. I almost met Lord Byron there, you know.'* These kinds of pictures are perfectly pleasant to many, and yes, of course it's impossible to capture something as intricately poetic as Venice in a painting. Perhaps if there was just one Canaletto painting of Venice – a big one with a resplendent sky above a festival taking place on the canals – I would bow down to it as a quiet masterpiece of observation. However, in their overproduction, formulaic qualities, and tendency to be displayed in gold frames in neat little rows, they lose mystery and relevance for me. Now that I think about it, Canaletto isn't really to blame: he had bills to pay like us, and there were no such things as museums when he was alive. He sent all his paintings off to their respective owners' country houses and didn't intend for them all to meet up one day in the Wallace Collection (a jewel box of a museum in London full of Canalettos and historical weapons) to irritate me in their aristocratic uniformity.

Just as I bring an artwork I love to life by my particular experience of it, I can also kill another one dead. By analysing what's happening, I don't just get to hone my experience of art, I also learn something about myself, or am reminded of something I hold to be a truth (in this case that Venice is unknowable in reproduction). But it doesn't always have to be a Freudian psychological voyage – not everything warrants the time. There is plenty of art in museums that will simply bore you and do little to excite you. That happens to me too. No one talks about it very much, but it's par for the course. Just keep moving.

IS IT ANNOYING?

Are you anxious that the artist is trying to pull the wool over your eyes? Perhaps it looks too thrown together and like the artist hasn't tried hard enough, or demonstrated a recognisable skill. For many people this was their response to hearing that Martin Creed won the Turner Prize in 2001 for an installation that the press described as a lightbulb going on and off. To be fair, the work *did* consist of an empty room with lightbulbs going on and off sporadically. As a young student spending most of my time looking, thinking, and writing about Italian Renaissance masters, I did think maybe he was having a laugh. But a fellow student far more conversant in conceptual art (art which prioritises the purity of ideas over the means in which it is made) pointed out to me that it was a brilliant play on minimalism. All painting must contend with capturing light of some form, and great art presents new ideas – isn't a lightbulb the ultimate symbol of a bright idea? Somehow in his repurposing of a household item, Creed had boiled down big concepts into something so small as to seem insignificant and even ridiculous at first.

Now, again, I am not here to make you love this work. Indeed I still don't *love* love it, but I have come to see it as a valid enterprise, and in its simplicity I believe it to possess a little lick of genius. Do I contend it can make many hearts soar on an aesthetic level? No, I don't. Back as a student I recognised that this was not Creed's intention. Rather I believed the opposite was true: he had no desire to make our heart soar, but wanted to ask why we expected an uplifting experience at all, to make us wonder *why* we assume that art must be beautiful or sensual rather than nimbly communicating an idea or a message.

For an increasing number of people going to see art these days, the art itself needn't possess buckets of beauty, sensuality, or aesthetic charm to engage them. Rather, it's paramount that the works provoke thought and operate with great originality. These are the people flocking to see work like *The Artist Is Present* by the performance artist Marina Abramović, who welcomed a record 850,000 visitors at the Museum of Modern Art in New York in 2010. For just under three months, she sat silently in a chair across from museum visitors, who took turns sitting in a chair positioned opposite her. The gift of the artist was time, space, energy, and a complete commitment to the situation she had staged. Many visitors cried unexpectedly during the encounter and found it to be profound and unforgettable. It is such a famous work now that I wish I could have experienced it first-hand, but of course, for many others this simply won't be appealing. If you fall into that camp when encountering a concept-driven work, don't feel as if you are other. There's no one right way, and prioritising a more literal aesthetic experience doesn't make you a villain!

IS IT TOO PRETTY?

'Decoration' is a bad word when it comes to art. I'll confess I get twitchy when someone mistakes my role as the curator for Soho House, a global private members' club for creatives, as being akin to an interior design initiative. I don't buy paintings to match the curtains and, perhaps slightly unreasonably, I'll fight to the death anyone who says that I do. Prettiness, which we might describe as the evil sister of decoration, can also be dangerous territory. It can seem too fluffy or unserious. If something is described as 'pretty', that might also mean it is not very original.

We've all seen those mass market canvases of gentle abstract marks in complementary colours. They are designed with an impossible expectation to appeal to everyone and thus make no impact at all. In my line of work, we call this 'bad hotel art' (in New York it's referred to as 'lobby art'). There is an element of snobbishness to this, which I have to take responsibility for. But, as someone who loves art, I feel that I am entitled to this opinion, just as a musician is allowed to say that they are depressed by elevator music. It's perfectly legitimate to think something is too pretty, too bland, or too uninspiring, and to demote it to decoration, just as elevator music is background noise to fill awkward silences in small spaces.

I love beautiful things, even pretty things, but I want them to stand apart, by which I mean I want to feel like they were made with meaning as opposed to being mass produced to be inoffensive and sell easily. Plenty of pretty or dangerously beautiful art will be likeable, even loveable, and you should feel no shame if that's your taste. I proudly love Dutch Golden Age floral still lifes, especially those by Rachel Ruysch, which are damn pretty.

With all these examples, my aim is to encourage you to give yourself permission to tune into your natural instincts around art. I want to help alleviate the feeling that, if you don't like something, either it is meaningless, or you are somehow deficient. But I also want to remind all of us that sometimes it is worthwhile pushing beyond that initial impression of disliking something or wanting to walk away in frustration. There are various levels of engagement with any kind of work of art. By asking yourself simple questions and paying attention to what you are seeing and feeling – even if it starts out negative or neutral – you have the opportunity to learn something about yourself. You might even change your initial impression – liking the piece more or less after giving it an enquiring once-over. Through this open and honest process, wherever you land once you step away, you will be able to better own your response. Even if your conclusion is that Canaletto is a genius!

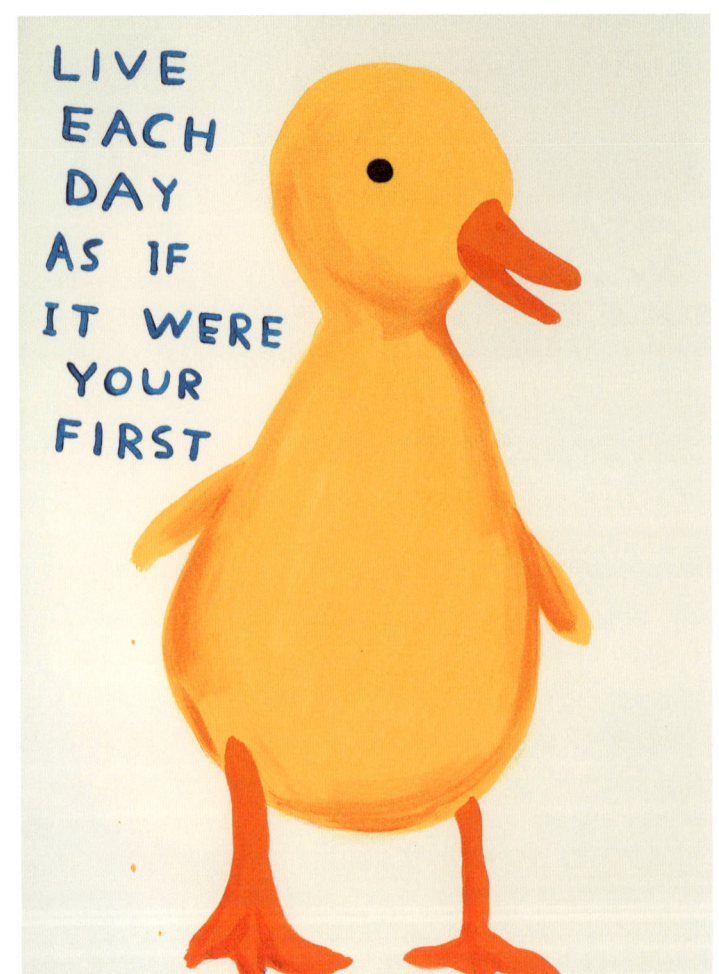

HOW TO ENJOY ART WITH CHILDREN - FOR ALL THE PARENTS AND CARERS OUT THERE

I completely understand why parents and carers will often put off taking young children to an art gallery or museum. We think of them as places designed for things not to be touched, and where you should not make a mess or be noisy – basically the opposite of what toddlers excel at. Despite this, every public gallery and museum is there for all of us: they operate as cultural community hubs and as such they *need* children as visitors. Many public institutions across the globe (in my experience France has a lot further to go and the UK is doing the best) are making excellent progress at actively factoring in the needs and experiences of children in their core activities. The Tate Modern in London is a great example: they programme their spaces for school holidays, once even turning the floor of the Turbine Hall into a giant collective crayon doodling board.

When I was on maternity leave, I loved taking my daughter to see art in galleries. They were excellent places to reconnect with the real world beyond the baby bubble. Going to galleries was a quiet, gentle re-entry into society, and they usually had excellent catering and bathroom facilities, both of which were very necessary at that time. I remember finding myself again; through the fog of exhaustion I would be enlivened by the displays, catching hold of an idea or thought unrelated to motherhood for the first time in weeks. I also felt calmer standing in front an artwork made decades or centuries ago by people who had made it through the life-altering chaos of parenthood, like the complex work engaging with themes of motherhood and the role of women in society by the late French artist Louise Bourgeois, or paintings by the seventeenth-century Dutch artist Johannes Vermeer, who had a casual fifteen children.

I'm pleased I went so much with a baby. It was good mental preparation for the next phase, when she was out of the sling or stroller and cleverly morphing into an independent and slightly terrifying human being who liked calling the shots despite lacking any experience of the world. I learned to relax into visits to galleries, keeping them short and, when I could, taking someone with me to occupy her so I might occasionally, heaven forbid, actually look at some art. When my daughter was about two and a half and becoming more verbal, I devised a system that was pretty foolproof. It worked in London's galleries, which I know very well, but crucially it also worked in galleries around the UK and overseas, meaning we could still take in culture when we were lucky enough to travel. I hope this system helps you to take a toddler to an art gallery: the more time they spend in these spaces when they're young, the less likely they are to feel isolated from the experience as they grow older – and the more you, as a parent or carer, may feel some moments of peace and a chance to connect with something beyond yourself.

TAKING A TODDLER TO A GALLERY

- Ensure the child in question is well rested, fed, and watered.

- Before you leave, write a simple checklist in colourful pens (with a nice big tick box next to each item) of things you are going to find at the gallery together. Bring a pencil (not a pen, unless you like to live dangerously) to tick them off. This should be enough to get you through at least a few rooms. If you are more organised than me, take a handy little clipboard.

- If it's a historic collection, you should be able to get all of these:

  – dog
  – lamb
  – horse
  – bird
  – baby
  – robes in their favourite colour

- blue sky with clouds
- bouquet of flowers
- wild-looking man
- sad-looking woman
- someone with no clothes on.

- If it's a contemporary collection, look out for these instead:

- dog-like shape
- child
- clothes in their favourite colour
- flowers
- wild-looking man
- sad-looking woman
- someone with no clothes on
- a rainbow
- a painting with dots
- a painting with stripes
- a big blob.

- Questions to ask throughout:

- What can you see? Describe the artwork to me.
- Do you like it?
- Which one do you think looks funny?
- Which one do you think looks a little scary?
- Which is the smallest/biggest/heaviest/bluest/ goldest?
- Which one do you want to take home?

- Which artwork looks most like mommy/daddy/ siblings/you?
- Can you draw your own on the back of our checklist?
- Where did you leave the checklist?
- Do you need a wee?

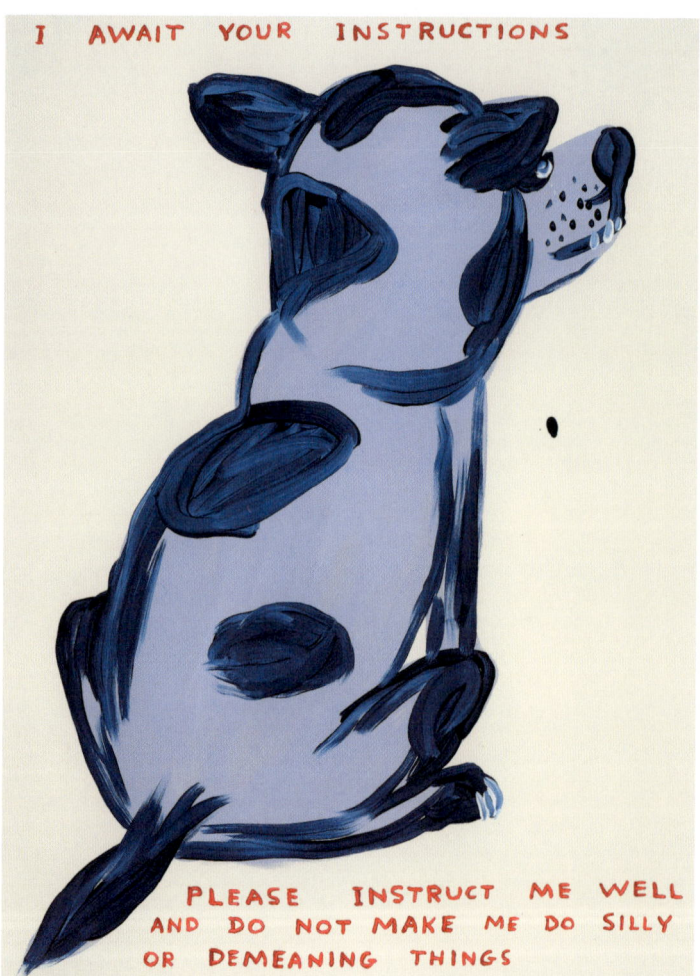

How to Make Your Dog More Cultural

It should be pretty obvious by now that I think the art world takes itself far too seriously: it does not have a reputation for being welcoming and fun. I think a great way to undermine the snootiness of art-world folk is to set about making your dog more cultural. With a dog as your companion, you are asserting a kind of 'take me as I am' attitude. Plus, as someone who is surrounded by dog lovers (including Mr Shrigley), it's important that people know they don't have to miss out on culture in favour of another woodland walk – there are plenty of places where you can include your four-legged friend.

The following tips are designed for dogs, but I suspect many could be adopted for a cat or other furry fella:

- I wouldn't suggest renaming your hound, but if the opportunity arises to name one from scratch, then it makes sense to give them a name that clearly conveys that this ain't no philistine pup. Take a trip to your local gallery and find a name that resonates. Personally I think that Rothko, Kahlo, and Riley all have great charm.

- In many parts of the world there are museums and galleries with extensive grounds. In South London, the gardens of the Horniman Museum boast some erudite-looking dogs. Also in London is an excellent public sculpture walk called the Line, which connects the Queen Elizabeth Olympic Park and the O2, is 4.8 miles long, and very much welcomes dogs. In New York there's an organisation called dOGUMENTA (a play on Documenta, the art gathering that happens every five years in Germany) that organises exhibitions for dogs – which is just about the most New York thing I have ever come across.

- Next time you visit a museum, take a detailed picture of all the animals you see. It's interesting to witness which types of art a dog can respond to by looking at photos on your phone. If you own a dog that howls at paintings of cats, you are doing brilliantly in your mission. It is fairly well demonstrated that dogs can recognise their owners in photographs and will also respond well to images of canines.

- Every city in the world features public art, from bold street art on the urban infrastructure to contemporary works that divide opinion to historic bronzes – usually fellas in military garb. These can all be enjoyed on four paws as well as two feet.

- When showing your dog art, it's useful to know they don't see as much colour as humans: they are limited to blue, yellow and shades of grey. They'll probably like a lot of David Shrigley's work, so you can show them this book if you'd like.

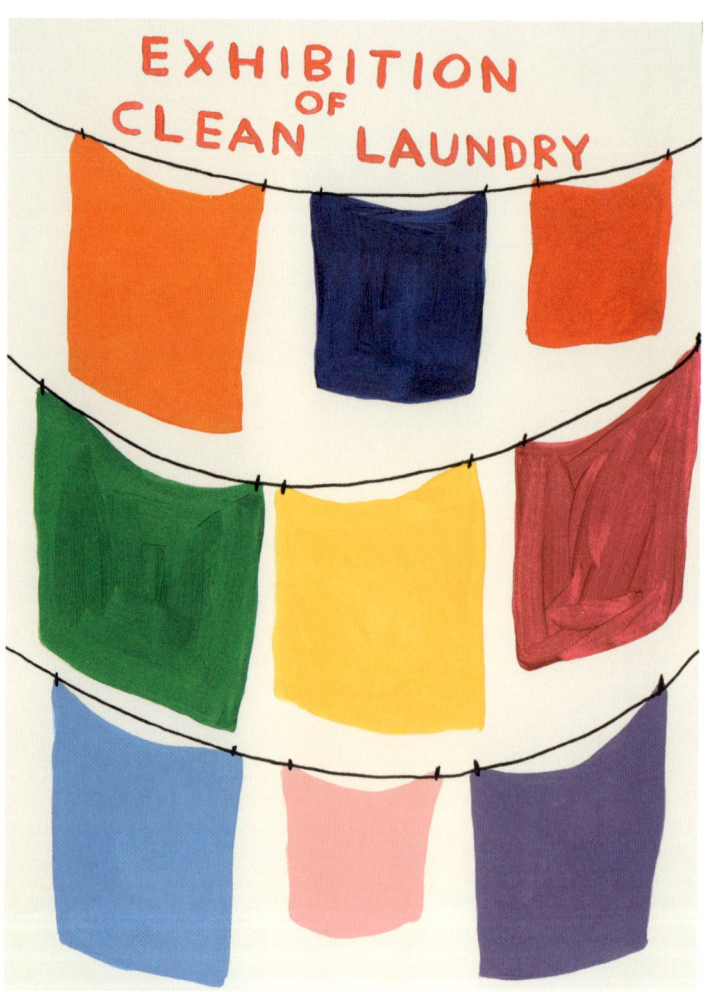

How to Art at Home

Aside from filling your home with your own art collection (which I thoroughly recommend; see Part Four for more), there are plenty of ways to have meaningful engagements with art at home. Art books are a natural place to start. But I completely understand why for most people, even those who self-describe as art lovers, picking up your average art history book can be off-putting. They are often theory-heavy and hard work. Some of the people who complain the loudest to me about art historical tomes are artists who would rather parade around the Tate naked than read T. J. Clark's Marxist interpretation of Impressionism.

When even the makers of art feel isolated from books about art, the rest of us can relax. However, it can be rewarding to find ways to engage with art without leaving the house. So what follow are my personal favourite ways to engage with art from the comfort of your sofa that are hopefully accessible, enjoyable, and even inspirational.

MOVIES

I do have a good list of starter books for you below, which I really rate for their fluency and openness. But just as was true for my high school essay on *Romeo and Juliet*, it's often more fun and faster to watch the movie.

99

So, here is a list of films that I love and that communicate something powerful, useful, and truthful about art or an artist.

The Thomas Crown Affair

I deliberated about whether to include this, as it includes so many dodgy painting reproductions. But ultimately I had to – as a teenager it was my first taste of the art world on screen, and it reeled me in like an art-hungry fish. Although I genuinely love *The Thomas Crown Affair* (specifically the 1999 remake), this movie has a lot to answer for – not just the gratuitous Rene Russo topless scene, but also the conceit that a billionaire would plot an art heist so he could live forever with his favourite painting. The truth about art heists is far less romantic: most stolen paintings end up being used as collateral or guarantees in organised crime drug deals.

Nonetheless, Pierce Brosnan's billionaire trying to outfox Russo's charismatic art insurance specialist in a cat-and-mouse game is scarily watchable, even for someone who knows better. The pacey gallery scene set to a Nina Simone track is a satisfying nod to René Magritte's *Man in a Bowler Hat* for art geeks. There is a lot of fantasy here, but at the core of *The Thomas Crown Affair* is a genuine love of art and what makes it so valuable beyond insurance records. Fun fact: the production's request to film at the Metropolitan Museum of Art in New York was flatly denied. No museum in the world wants to advertise how to rob it.

Frida

Frida Kahlo is one of the most instantly recognisable artists on the planet. Even in cities she never visited and where there isn't any of her artwork on display you can buy candles or cushions with her distinctive face on it. She's become emblematic of her home country, Mexico, and might be the only woman artist that most people can name (I hope that this expands to many more names in my lifetime). She was no doubt already incredibly well known, both in Mexico and beyond, but the 2002 biopic *Frida*, starring Salma Hayek as Frida, helped bring her to even larger audiences. The movie largely focuses on her tumultuous marriage with the artist Diego Rivera but it's faithful enough to her story and draws out the miraculous way art can offer salvation to its maker.

Mr Turner

Mike Leigh's film about J. M. W. Turner is not your average artist biopic. It's a visual feast with a compelling and well-researched narrative that traces the poignant last twenty-five years of the artist's life. I love that the lead actor Timothy Spall learned to paint for real to play Turner, a performance he followed up by playing another British artist, L. S. Lowry, in *Mrs Lowry & Son*, and then got so hooked he developed his own painting practice.

BOOKS

Having cherished the few art books I had as a young person, I think perhaps I had started to take them a bit for granted as my adult home filled up with them. But during the COVID-19 pandemic they once again became a lifeline for me. Every few days, I would place a different book on the kitchen table and hope it would drag my attention away from the rollercoaster of boredom, anxiety, and frustration. I loved how the books got their hooks into me, how one minute I would be doom-scrolling and the next I would emerge from looking at Hockney's vibrant, expressionistic landscapes feeling just that little bit better about the world (especially when I brought to mind the title of the book he released with writer Martin Gayford, *Spring Cannot Be Cancelled*).

I am a hoarder of art books, so creating a shortlist was a horrible task – especially as there has been an explosion of great art publishing in the past decade, with more books than ever before designed to appeal to a wider audience and to revise who and what is included in the story of art. A very good way to get a sense of what is on offer is to go in person to a public art gallery's bookshop and do some browsing, but here are some books that I think are enjoyable places to begin.

Ferren Gipson's *The Ultimate Art Museum*

Gipson, an art historian keen to revise art history to be more inclusive, has built an imaginary museum with no restrictions on time and space. Instead it's a compendium of treasure after treasure with a lively, easy-to-navigate design. It's beautiful to flick through at random for inspiration, but also educational. I often gift this to teenage art addicts as their first art history book.

E. H. Gombrich's *The Story of Art*
Gombrich is the OG of art history. He published this book in 1950 and it was an instant classic, in many ways setting the canon of art from ancient to modern. There are passages of writing that are so dazzling, yet lucid, that they made me fall in love with works I used to dislike. A product of its time, it did not include any women artists, which was addressed by the best-selling 2022 riposte, *The Story of Art Without Men* by Katy Hessel.

Sarah Thornton's *Seven Days in the Art World*
This is easily my favourite book about the contemporary art world. It's not written by an art historian but rather by a cultural sociologist who presents day-in-the-life narratives in distinct settings such as an art fair, an artist studio, and an auction house. She is gentle but honest about the art world's peccadillos and thinly veiled obsession with money and status. It's bursting with insider knowledge and would be indispensable to anyone who wanted to work or engage with the contemporary art world.

PODCASTS
Talk Art
Presented by the art dealer Robert Diament and the actor and art enthusiast Russell Tovey, these two charmers host an art-world guest on each episode, usually an artist but

sometimes an art historian such as myself. Tovey keeps the conversation down to earth, while Diament brings a heartfelt passion for every guest, which is infectious.

The Week in Art and *A Brush With . . .*

The Art Newspaper is the journal of record for the art world. While its print and online editions might still be very much industry-focused, its podcasts, hosted by seasoned art journalist Ben Luke, are more accessible. Each episode of *The Week in Art* usually covers two timely art stories, provides a news round-up, and ends with the work of the week, an in-depth look at often-unexpected artworks with an expert guest. Its sister podcast, *A Brush With . . .*, hosts a distinguished artist in every episode for a deep dive into their career.

The Missing Madonna

I hope there will be more podcasts like *The Missing Madonna*, a mini-series from the BBC that recounts the brazen theft of a masterpiece by Leonardo from a castle in Scotland in 2003. Involving some likely lads from Liverpool and the criminal underworld, the show is hosted by Olivia Graham, who has a personal connection to the story that makes the whole case come alive. The BBC also created *The Banksy Story*, which did little to shed light on who the anonymous street artist is, but absolutely delivers on his rise to international fame and his obsessive fanbase.

MAGAZINES

Art magazines tend to be very industry-centric. The most famous is *Art Forum*, which tends to be about 80 per cent glossy adverts and 20 per cent dense art speak. *The Art Newspaper* is more readable, but I doubt anyone who isn't already seriously engaged in the business of art would get much out of it. Thankfully museum magazines, originally designed to entice membership and advertise museum events, are now stepping in to fill the void with clear, engaging, and accessible content. *RA Magazine* from the UK's Royal Academy and *Tate Etc* are two excellent examples. These magazines are sent to you if you buy an annual membership to the respective museums (really worth it if you plan on seeing more than two exhibitions a year, as they grant free access to all exhibitions too). Otherwise, you can buy individual issues in the museum stores or online.

DOCUMENTARIES

The Price of Everything
Much like *Seven Days in the Art World*, this feature-length documentary goes behind closed doors to unpick how art is sold, priced, and marketed. It follows some brilliant characters, from auction house gurus to long-forgotten artists, and makes for a poetic reflection on the funny old business of art. You can rent *The Price of Everything* on Amazon or YouTube.

The Andy Warhol Diaries

I devour art documentaries, and this is probably my favourite one. The premise sounds dubious – Andy Warhol's extensive diaries narrated by an AI-generated Warhol voice – but the result is uncanny and incredible. Vast quantities of archival footage and fascinating talking heads of people who knew the artist and his circle personally bring Warhol back from the dead. There are six episodes, each around an hour long, and yet I still wanted more. Netflix, who released this in 2022, ought to be screening more ambitious art content like this.

WEBSITES

When I first started working in the art world it was incredibly unusual to be able to google a living artist who was not a major museum-level name: there would seemingly be no trace of them. The British artistic duo Rob and Nick Carter told me that when they created their website in the early noughties, they were among the first artists to do so in their peer group, and Damien Hirst used to mockingly call them 'RobandNick.com' as a result. But it didn't take long for artists to realise that an online presence would become critical to their success.

Around the same time, pioneering websites like *Artnet* began to emerge, which disrupted the opaque nature of auction sales by listing auction results (for a subscription fee). I benefitted hugely in the early days of my career from *The Art Story*, which is a free encyclopaedic art resource for established artists that in my view is still yet to be rivalled for its in-depth commentary. For contemporary artists, a huge shift happened when *Artsy* was launched. It may not have been entirely successful in its endeavour to create an online art market, but it has become an unrivalled resource to see the profile of contemporary artists, such as their price point, sold works at auction, and which galleries have worked with them. Emerging artists (those in the first few years of their practice) will not appear on Artsy because they have yet to make enough waves to get noticed. For more general art writing, the website of the Museum of Modern Art in New York has superb online content.

I end this chapter with a suggestion to devour what I think is one of the greatest achievements of the digital age (alongside *Chicken Shop Date*): Google Arts & Culture. It's nice to give an underdog like Google a shout out; I hope they do well. Jokes aside, Google Arts & Culture is a game changer. As I write, I am looking in microscopic detail at the surface of van Gogh's *Sunflowers*. It's not better than seeing it in person, but it's a tremendous tool that allows for the kind of close look that would get you arrested in the gallery: you can trace every brushstroke, every crack in the surface. Through the initiative's remarkable high-quality imaging, you can get nose to nose with the world's greatest art. What follows in the next chapter is an in-depth consideration of three artworks, including *Sunflowers*, which you will be able to bring to mind instantly, but which, as I explain, are worth putting effort into looking at again.

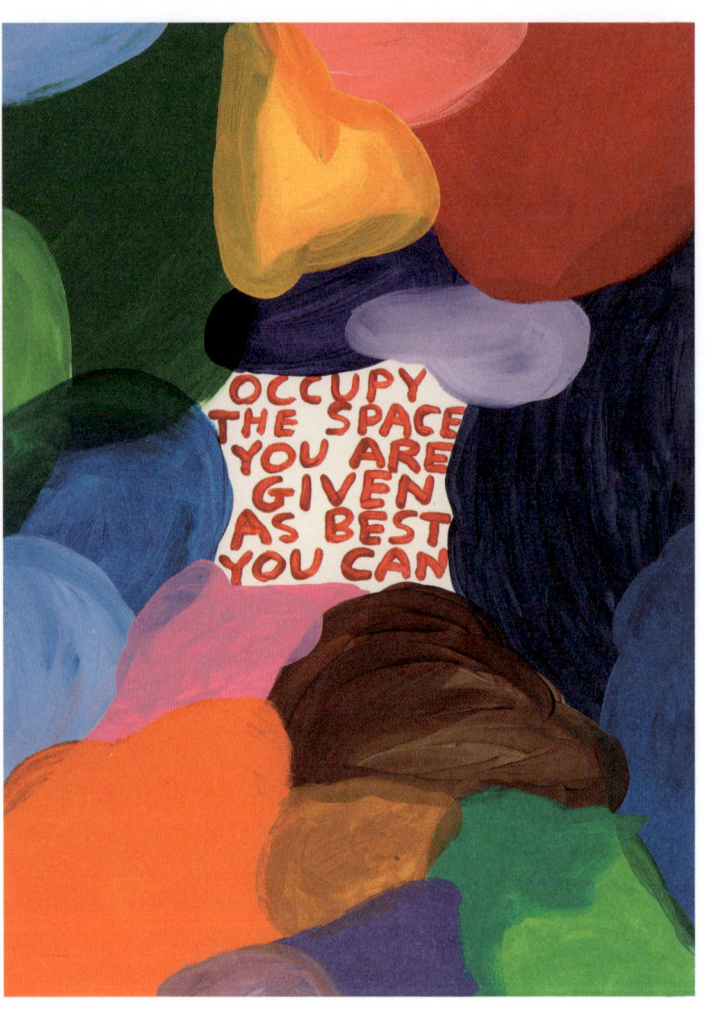

HOW TO ENJOY ICONIC ARTWORK

There are a select number of artworks that are part of our shared cultural consciousness. I have picked three that are so famous, so visited, and so talked about that they are known the world over and discussed in the same way as extraordinary places of natural beauty like the Grand Canyon or the Great Barrier Reef. It's not difficult to find them – society sort of shoves them in your face. They are iconic, and with good reason. But that icon status very often causes problems for the viewer.

What follows is some homework, of sorts, before you tackle these bona fide masterpieces. If I think seeing art should be as easy as listening to a new album or watching *Squid Game* on Netflix (I really need to get round to doing that), then why do I want you to do some prep work? Because these works have transcended their maker, geography, and materials to become benchmarks for Western culture, and that's an awful lot to live up to. As concepts, they have already found firm lodging in our minds before we even get within a mile of them, and when you have such high expectations it's understandable to not really 'see' them properly.

The problem is partly that their fame means crowds, queues, and hype, which all too often can cause disappointment. I understand why so many people guiltily whisper that the *Mona Lisa* was a let-down, that she's too small and too far away, and why when people go to the Sistine Chapel, they mostly remember being yelled at not to take photos. These artworks are sometimes treated simply as sightseeing landmarks – people might 'tick off' van Gogh's *Sunflowers* in much the same way as nearby Trafalgar Square.

Although I can't do much about the viewing conditions or the touristic element of each of these artworks, I can help with some small hacks to improve your chances of getting the supernatural experience that is in touching distance.

MICHELANGELO'S SISTINE CHAPEL VATICAN MUSEUMS, ROME

Before you go
Rewatch *Good Will Hunting*. This is always a good idea, but I suggest it here because I love that tiny moment when Robin Williams' character, Sean, shuts down a lippy Will played by Matt Damon. He's only read about the world, never truly experienced it, and a fast way to exploit this weakness is for Sean to point out that Will, for all his book smarts, has never stepped foot inside the Vatican: 'But I'll bet you can't tell me what it smells like in the Sistine Chapel. You've never actually stood there and looked up at that beautiful ceiling.'

Think of this sentiment about the power of reality as you walk down the last flight of dingy steps, because you are about to be changed. You won't be able to go back to being Will Hunting, because you will always have seen the Sistine Chapel, and therefore seen and *felt* something that set a new standard not just for art, but for what humankind could achieve.

That ceiling is all the work of one very special artist, Michelangelo, whose feet touched this very same beautiful marble floor you are about to tread upon too. Upon entering the Chapel, which remains the place that every new Pope is elected and thus is extremely sacred for Catholics, be aware that you are about to see an incredible smorgasbord of art. As a young undergraduate on a trip to Rome, I sort of washed up into the chapel, deposited in an overbearing wave of tourists. I took some time to get my bearings because it was such a feast for the eyes; I even nervously laughed aloud, as I felt like Alice falling down the rabbit hole and arriving in a Renaissance wonderland. Like Alice, I wasn't entirely at ease, because I was so unprepared and overawed. What awaits every visitor is a cornucopia, something that made me feel small by contrast to its abundance. I felt like my body was ill designed to be able to take it all in – I wanted it all at once, but I couldn't have it. My neck instantly craned back to take in the most famous ceiling in the world.

What makes it so special

The ceiling of the Sistine Chapel is an icon of the Italian Renaissance that was begun in 1508. Michelangelo, a stubborn and brilliant man, spent four years painting this ceiling (he saved time by not washing very much, but let's not dwell on his less than perfumed feet, which were so stinky that they are actually recorded in art history). The fact that Michelangelo created this masterpiece is, in many ways, astonishing. Not only did he consider himself a sculptor – and most certainly *not* a painter – he had likely also never previously created a fresco (a tricky kind of mural painted on a fresh plaster surface to cement the pigment into the wall). To have pulled this off is akin to winning the Tour de France the first time you rode a bike. Any other artist would have enlisted a team of assistant artists to tackle such a gargantuan and complex fresco, but Michelangelo sacked the initial assistants he hired and then went it alone.

There are over 300 figures on the ceiling, a ceiling which is around the size of two tennis courts. Every one of those figures has a distinct pose and attitude. Michelangelo made every other artist before him – artists who, almost exclusively, repeated figures and faces with only mild variations – look like they had been phoning it in. The ceiling is broken into various sections, each depicting different stories from the Old Testament, as well as portraying individual prophets in little pointed niches. The body language and postures of these individuals, such as Jonah and Daniel, are astoundingly realistic. Some of them look like they are sitting courtside at a basketball game, transfixed by what's happening, with the most marvellous jutting-out knees.

The most famous part is the central image, depicting the creation of mankind by God. This is a completely radical pictorial invention. Michelangelo takes a few simple sentences from the Book of Genesis and communicates them to us in a vivid, unforgettable scene. Adam is recumbent, splendidly ripped, nude. He is about to receive the spark of life from God, who rocks up on a cloud. Their fingers, though outstretched towards each other, do not touch. In this gap between them is the difference between the idea of humankind and the red-blooded reality of it: every book ever written, every film made, every city built, every child born, every single human endeavour, and all of our mistakes lie in the empty space. The whole show of life is about to begin.

The sheer originality of this cannot be overemphasised. In art, the Christian God before had always been dial-a-beard, but now here he is conjuring, building, and inspiring. It's a radical way to imagine the beginnings of humankind, and reminds me of the poetic manner in which Michelangelo talked about his great passion: stone carving. He described every block of marble as having been granted a divine artistic treasure and it was simply his job as the sculptor to release God's creation from the stone (perhaps Michelangelo invented the humblebrag too). In this sense, Adam – who looks like one of Michelangelo's other iconic creations, the fabulously jacked sculpture of David in Florence – is like a dormant figure being liberated from marble into flesh. It is not just the virtuoso paint handling and realism that makes this such an outstanding artwork, it is Michelangelo's inventive intellectual rigour. He creates a bridge to the divine for non-believers, and even for contemporary religious cynics his work has an uncanny ability to transmit huge intellectual concepts.

Michelangelo was thirty-three when he started the ceiling, a task that we know from his letters he found physically exhausting and torturous in its complexity. Somewhat reluctantly, he returned to the Sistine Chapel to paint the altar wall nearly twenty-five years later for another Pope (he worked in the service of nine in total, more than any other artist in history). Older and jaded from his turbulent times (he heard first-hand accounts of the Sack of Rome in 1527, which was like hell on earth), his later creation depicts the Last Judgment. He dropped the comic-strip-like division of scenes he had devised for the ceiling and made one big writhing, whirling scene in which the trumpets sound and the dead who have been knocking around Purgatory rise up and are told their fate. Will they descend into the terrifying dark bowels of hell or be released into the heavenly blue skies above?

In Michelangelo's time, the concept of atoning for one's sins and being ready to face judgement from God in the afterlife was so real as to be a daily preoccupation. An entire industry had sprung up to offer fast-track salvation, eerily similar to today's wellness trends that promise to deliver us from ourselves. Michelangelo was a devout man, probably so devout he stayed celibate to abate his passion for men, and as he aged, we can witness in his letters, drawings, and poetry how possessed he became with meeting his maker.

His vision of the Last Judgment is all about the body: we see saints perched on clouds with the instruments of their martyrdom – Saint Lawrence with the grill, Saint Catherine with her wheel. Their gruesome endings are otherwise a distant memory: their bodies show no scars, as if by walking in the light of God they have been made perfect again. Michelangelo also shows us how the body might misbehave. Tormented figures try to wrestle their way up to heaven – the damned ain't gonna go down without a fight, and we feel the weight of their bodies fighting both gravity and eternal damnation. It's a psychological minefield, a perpetual nightmare in which no one looks happy – even the saints look on edge, and the Virgin Mary practically cowers as her son powerfully unleashes his judgement. So, when the Vatican guards are repeating, 'Silenzio'/'No photo', just think: it could be worse.

Timing

The busiest time to go to the Vatican is Monday. It is closed on Sundays (except for the very busy last Sunday of the month, when entry is free) and so every poor soul who didn't realise will turn up the next day. Always pre-book. It's absolutely worth the extra money to get the pre-9am morning slot, getting in at 7:30am after a double espresso. Don't dilly-dally: go straight to the Sistine Chapel (try not to mow anyone down on your speed walk – it is, after all, a sacred place). After you've experienced it, in the most quiet that will be available all day, you can double back to enjoy the other parts of the Vatican people flock to: the Belvedere Courtyard (home to nothing short of the finest ancient marble sculptures such as *Laocoön and His Sons*); the gardens (if they are good enough for the Pope to forget his troubles in they'll work for us); Raphael's Rooms (signposted as 'Stanze di Raffaello'), known for the amazing frescoes by this other great Renaissance painter; and the art gallery, the Pinacoteca, where you will see other classic works, like one of my favourite Caravaggio paintings, *The Deposition*. But I also grant you permission to only go to the Sistine Chapel. It's worth the money and, as with food, art gorging is a bad idea: even if it is world class, consume too much and chances are you'll end the day feeling sick.

Pssst: perhaps even better than the early slot, in the summer the Vatican is open late on Fridays. The Sistine Chapel gets quiet after about 7:30pm until closing, meaning you don't have to rush. The third best option is Wednesday towards the end of the afternoon, as there tend to be fewer tourists mid-week.

MONA LISA, LOUVRE, PARIS

Before you go

Don't bother reading an expert's tome on this most famous of paintings, even though there are loads to choose from. Instead, watch Beyoncé and Jay-Z's (credited as The Carters) magnificent music video 'Apeshit' directed by Ricky Saiz. It was filmed after-hours in an empty Louvre Museum and delights in the cultural phenomenon that is a five-centuries-old, 77 cm x 53 cm piece of poplar wood with some oil paint on it, which has demanded the attention of people the world over for hundreds of years. She may not have transfixed everyone who ever saw her – I am talking about *Mona Lisa*, not Beyoncé, here – but that doesn't mean you don't need to see this painting. Yes, people complain she is too hard to get a good look at. And it is true that, so priceless is she, that she is kept at a distance of a few metres from the public, imprisoned behind thick bulletproof glass. But that is not her fault.

What I love about the music video is that it does something clever, linking a global contemporary cultural icon (Beyoncé) to an historic cultural object that is synonymous with the word 'masterpiece'. The video also allow you to see the details of the painting and how it looks in an empty space, which is impossible for nearly everyone – except Beyoncé. Having established a night-time setting, opulent and atmospheric with ornate ceilings, footsteps echo off-camera and then, all of a sudden, we are plunged into a gallery where two figures lean against a railing in front of a portrait (even the Carters can't get past the rail). Before we see a close up of the two mega-star's faces, we get a lingering shot of *La Giaconda*, which is what the French and Italians call the *Mona Lisa*.

Of all the paintings on display at the Louvre, or indeed round the world, the Carters choose to stand on either side of her frame. They are announcing a shared greatness, a shared power, an unrivalled status as global icons. No other painting would have been able to perform such a gargantuan task. The *Mona Lisa* broadcasts ultimate cultural authority, and in turn Beyoncé and Jay-Z make this 500-year-old portrait all the more relevant. After six minutes of completely brilliant choreography and tableau-style set-ups throughout the museum – taking in some bangers like Théodore Géricault's enormous painting *The Raft of the Medusa*, as well as some iconic ancient sculptures such as the *Venus de Milo*, we return to Leonardo's more modestly sized painting. The Carters slowly turn from us to look at her. Smaller the *Mona Lisa* may be, but it is the grand finale; hers is the last face we see.

The video is a thrilling meeting between today's pop culture and an artwork that has been a permanent anchor in human history for five centuries. Watching it before you go to the Louvre can help you to think about what you'll be part of when you're there, sharing in the phenomenon that is the *Mona Lisa*. You will be the latest in a long line of people to have made a pilgrimage to this work: kings, queens, emperors, presidents, and Beyoncé have stood where you will stand.

Of course, she's still small, and it will still be crowded, and she'll still be behind bulletproof glass. Why is it exactly that the *Mona Lisa* is the Top Trump in art? Isn't her fame a bit mysterious? Are we being manipulated to adhere to the cult? Does her status eclipse everything else, making it impossible to assess whether this really is 'the greatest work of art ever made'? When I first went to the Louvre, I had recently graduated from university and expected to walk in and be able to commune immediately with the most famous painting in the world. I know I am not alone in feeling like a fraud. I felt isolated from the painting's greatness, and mostly I was irritated by the crowds – and this was in a pre-camera phone era. I was embarrassed at my disappointment. I hadn't expected to be so distracted by the hoopla, though maybe this is what it was like to try to listen to the Beatles play at the height of their fame – you could only hear the screaming.

But I kept going back and talking about how I felt with my colleagues (art geeks have gossipy watercooler chat about paintings, by the way). Now, I can focus on what got the *Mona Lisa* to where she is. Whether it's your first visit or your fifth, I want to help you separate the fame from the frame.

What makes it so special

Leonardo's *Mona Lisa* is the very definition of iconic, but there was no grand unveiling in his life to signal the birth of her cult status. As was almost always the way with this most brilliant but easily distracted of geniuses, Leonardo didn't complete the work on time (it took ten years!) and moreover it didn't stay with the family who commissioned it in about 1503. The *Mona Lisa* was commissioned by a Florentine silk merchant named Francesco del Giocondo (hence her Italian name, *La Gioconda*), who requested a portrait of his wife, Lisa Gherardini. She's called 'Mona Lisa' as a shortened version of 'Ma Donna' – my lady.

But rather than giving it to them, even though it was ten years late, we can assume Leonardo rather liked the work, as he took it with him when he went to work for the King of France. And in France it remained, for a while adorning Napoleon's bedroom wall. It was a much-copied image, even in his lifetime – one of my favourites is a 1505 pen-and-ink copy by fellow Teenage Mutant Ninja Turtle, Raphael, also in the Louvre collection. Giorgio Vasari, the first art historian and Leonardo's near-contemporary, wrote in *The Lives of the Artists* in 1550, 'Looking at this face, anyone who wanted to know how far nature can be imitated by art would understand immediately . . . all will acknowledge that the execution of this painting is enough to make the strongest artist tremble with fear.'

There's no doubt the work was special when Leonardo made it, not just for his enigmatic style, which we will come onto, but also for its new approach to composition. Leonardo does away with a profile portrait (i.e. side-on), which he probably thought had been done to death. Instead, he presents the sitter in a three-quarter pose, with one shoulder closer to us and one receding into the background. This gives her a remarkably animated quality, as if she just sat down and turned to face the artist. A true Renaissance man with fingers in many pies – including designing parachutes and helicopters – Leonardo was an 'artist inventor' who loved to experiment with his paint. He developed a technique called sfumato, which for me feels like seeing all his pictures in a smoke-filled jazz club. By using multiple layers of glaze with lots of linseed oil and not much pigment, he created a soft-focus picture with no sharp edges, no lines to speak of: everything is blended and wispy and fuzzy and lovely.

He also positioned his subject high up above the land-scape below her, something I have always gotten a kick out of, as she appears like a deity presiding over her kingdom. It was also a daring picture for its age because Mona Lisa makes eye contact with all her viewers. Having seen so many women portrayed looking demurely down at their cross stitch or whatever symbol of unthreatening femininity has been thrust upon them, it's refreshing that the most famous subject in art history is a normal woman who happily holds the world's gaze. Because, of course, she is not a deity or even a queen: she is a bourgeois wife in her mid-twenties, sitting for a painting commissioned by her husband. She remains with us, a forthright presence, conscious of being looked at, and with eyes so lifelike it feels like they do indeed follow you across the room.

And yes, there's that smile. It's like she is sharing a joke with Leonardo, or like they are both in on a secret together. In its subtlety, it is completely unforgettable. She doesn't look daft, as most people do in smiling portraits (which are rare because they are so hard to achieve), and neither does she look sarcastic. Instead, she looks as if she is really smiling, just for us as she did for Leonardo. This realism lends the painting a fantastic psychological depth. For as long as the *Mona Lisa* has existed, viewers have connected with it and felt like they somehow knew this woman.

Now, of course, we all do know her, even if just from adverts: she is a benchmark of Western culture. But when you stand in front of the real thing, you have a chance to really look at what it is about that face that connects. There have been countless speculations about this painting. One theory diagnoses her with a glandular condition and the other posits that the work portrays

Leonardo's male assistant, Salai, in drag. Stranger yet is the analysis by art historian Silvano Vinceti, who used magnified high-resolution images, and believes there are microscopic letters and numbers in the eyes and background.

While I am cynical about the obsession with 'decoding' Leonardo's artworks, as if he were some kind of time traveller waiting for a computer-game generation to be born who could unlock the ciphers he left us, I do think he intentionally took this work beyond a straightforward portrait. He was a pioneer, grappling with the big questions of his time, and I believe he set out to make a special picture that would astonish audiences.

X-rays reveal that Leonardo modified the clothing to make it less time-specific; she wears just a simple dress and no jewels. He abstracts the details of her appearance and removes the specificity of the background. He blended various carefully observed landscapes, including features such as a river and a bridge, but resisted allowing the background to represent one single place. Hands were rarely so prominently on display in Italian portraits, and would normally have been holding a symbolic religious object or in a position of prayer. In the *Mona Lisa*, her hands are left empty and have no obvious function. They contribute to the lack of specificity and enhance the sense that we are having an unmediated encounter – details and ornaments do not get in the way. Don't be mistaken for thinking

Leonardo neglected to paint her eyebrows for the same principle: they were there originally but have been worn away over time.

Over the long period he worked on this portrait, Leonardo laboured to paint something that we can read (a portrait), but that remains undefined and unknowable (what is she thinking; where is she?). Leonardo poured his staggering knowledge of optics, philosophy, and anatomy into the work, to go beyond his portrait commission and achieve something that grasps at the metaphysical. In other words, the *Mona Lisa* is intentionally mystical: it explores how we see and who we are, something that gets to the nature of existence. It is as if it is a collective portrait of humankind within the natural world, a gentle smiling force who looks at us as much as we look at her.

The cult that has taken hold may well be a sign that Leonardo was successful in his endeavour. So famous is this face that bones have been exhumed, the Kennedys threw the painting a dinner party at the White House, and biologists have spent years studying the precise details of that smile. To take nothing away from what a beguiling artwork it is, it is also true that a large part of the *Mona Lisa*'s global status today is thanks to a diminutive Italian named Vincenzo Peruggia. He entered the Louvre in August 1911 wearing a technician's overcoat to blend in with staff and then he casually took the Leonardo off the four pins that held it to the wall, wrapped it in his overcoat, and walked out with the masterpiece. Heads rolled at the museum, which closed for a week in a state of emergency that led to an unprecedented kind of public cultural mourning. The painting was on the front cover of newspapers and fast became a household name across France, Italy, and beyond. The story kept momentum as the investigation continued, including treating Pablo Picasso as a suspect in the theft.

Leonardo's work suffered the indignity of spending two years in a trunk hidden in the thief's small Parisian apartment. Peruggia was finally caught in 1913, as he tried to flog the work to an art dealer in Florence, and begged clemency as his motive was to return the painting to Italy as a 'generous act of patriotism'. Through all of this, the painting's fame grew far beyond the relatively small circle of art-world cognoscenti who had previously marvelled at Leonardo's achievement: now the public was engaged and would flock to the empty spot in the museum, enjoying the grim spectacle of its absence.

When it was rediscovered in Florence, the painting enjoyed a short period of triumphant display in its home country for the first and last time in its life, with hundreds of thousands of people coming to see a portrait of a long-dead Florentine woman who was now something of an icon far beyond the confines of art history. Since then, the cult has only grown, as she became swept up in the twentieth century's taste for image consumption and brand making – she remains the most used artwork in advertising history. She is both a symbol of mass tourism and a warning about a globalised world, where a work of art can be overwhelmed by visitors.

The problem with this frenzied attention is that it has become hard to make your own connection to something so commodified, packaged, and signposted. Your voice gets small, because millions of people have already seen the *Mona Lisa* and spoken for you. But be more Beyoncé. When you are walking into the Louvre, whether it's the first or fifth time you have seen the *Mona Lisa*, take your moment to look with *your* eyes, to connect with the object and not just the cult. The legend got you here, but now it is your turn to be present, to look, feel, engage. I always try to pause to notice five specific things about the work before moving on or getting my phone out to take a photo. Think of it like a moment to retune the radio: you need to fade out the noise and settle into your private channel, even if just for a couple of minutes.

After the selfie (we've all done it), head down the hall to take in the other masterpiece by Leonardo hiding in plain sight, the 'Lonely Leonardo' as I call it. The *Virgin of the Rocks* depicts two fleshy toddlers – the infant Christ and St John the Baptist – meeting in an incredibly moody, rocky landscape, which gives the picture its unusual name. Looking at this painting, I see an artist who used art historical conventions (religious stories and portrait commissions) to pole vault into a new pictorial terrain – one of deeply atmospheric, mysterious, potent, and never fully knowable scenes. Nowhere else in the world would a top-notch and large Leonardo painting sit so unvisited.

Timing

The Louvre is always busy. It is busier still when it offers rare free visiting windows, such as all day on 14 July (Bastille Day) and after 6pm on the first Friday of the month. A good option is the end of the afternoon mid-week. You can actually have a grand old time in the Louvre with just one hour, and far fewer people arrive at 5pm than at 9am. The Louvre is open late every Wednesday and Friday (but be cautious on the first Friday of the month) and much like the Vatican's summer late sessions, this is your chance to beat the mega crowds.

In any event, always go straight to the *Mona Lisa*. It's tragically signposted everywhere, with little photos of it pointing the way like a spectacle at a circus. I think that these small, dreadful reproductions dampen the whole experience no end: you've seen a bad version of the painting ten times before you finally find it, so do your best to ignore them. There is talk of building a separate entrance and underground chamber for the painting. I am sure Veronese, a Venetian master who currently shares the room with the *Mona Lisa*, would be delighted: despite being a legend, he's nothing but wallpaper for Leonardo's little grenade of a picture.

VAN GOGH'S SUNFLOWERS
NATIONAL GALLERY, LONDON

Before you go

There are probably more films and television programmes about Vincent van Gogh than about any other artist in history. So, you can hold a van Gogh viewing marathon from the comfort of your home before you even arrive at the National Gallery. The most famous van Gogh films are *Lust For Life* (1956), *Loving Vincent* (2017), and *At Eternity's Gate* (2018). However, I think the most compelling use of your time is a succinct three-minute clip on the *Doctor Who* channel on YouTube called 'Vincent van Gogh Visits the Gallery'. This is an excerpt of the BBC's long-standing and hugely popular sci-fi television show about a time-travelling 2,000-year-old Doctor. In this episode, the Doctor and van Gogh visit a gallery where people are enjoying van Gogh's art. A curator (played by Bill Nighy) gives a rousing overview of the unsurpassed legacy of the great van Gogh, without knowing that a time-travelling Vincent is listening while crying tears of joy.

Van Gogh is about as mainstream as artists come. He is known the world over as the painter of *Sunflowers*, but also as a tragic figure who mutilated his ear and whose work was misunderstood in his lifetime only to sell for tens of millions long after his suicide. His most expensive artwork to date is *Orchard with Cypresses*, which sold for $117.2 million at Christie's in New York in 2022. Crucially, in the *Doctor Who* clip, there is no talk of money. Vincent does not cry because his work generates enormous sums in an auction room. He was already a household name by the time his paintings started to break world auction records.

Rather, he is moved by the fact that the public are deeply touched by his art, that his message finally landed and remains with us. When you visit, remember that it is not an accident that people the world over have a special relationship with this painting and his work more widely. Van Gogh purposefully endeavoured to create artworks that directly communicated with the viewer, that clearly expressed enduring human themes such as hope, love, anguish, and suffering. Today we expect artists to want to reach their audience, to think about us as they create, but this was by no means typical before him.

I don't think I would be writing this book if it were not for van Gogh. Not only is he the artist who helped me to fall madly in love with art as a child, but also he is the artist whom I know I can talk to anyone about because his life and his work are so famous. This gargantuan fame, however, can sometimes act as a shadow looming over an iconic painting like *Sunflowers* – we run the risk of looking at his paintings only through the prism of his biography. The general perception is one of constant suffering, and often he is cast as a wild man (they even call him wild in *Doctor Who*) who made art in a deranged frenzy. Nothing could be further from the truth. He was a sensitive, educated man who spoke and read several languages and made his plentiful masterpieces between bouts of mental illness. Art was a salvation for him, and he believed it should be a tonic for us all.

What makes it so special?
Sunflowers is certainly a tonic. After World War 2, the painting became a star attraction at a 1947 landmark retrospective of Van Gogh's work at what is today known as Tate Britain. After the gallery welcomed an astonishing 5,000 visitors a day, it wrote to the Arts Council requesting funds as the floorboards had been worn out. We also know that the priceless work of art was transferred from its normal position in the National Gallery on Trafalgar Square to Pimlico for this exhibition in the back of a black cab! Today, such a move would be taken with the strictest of security measures. Despite its humble journey, it quickly became emblematic of the post-war period, a kind of beacon of hope as Europe rebuilt itself.

If we can try to set aside the painting's stupendous international fame for a moment, on the surface, *Sunflowers* is a pretty straightforward picture – especially compared with the other two artworks I have picked out as shared cultural benchmarks. While Michelangelo's Sistine Chapel frescoes are enormous and visually complex and Leonardo's *Mona Lisa* is enigmatic and comes with its own dramatic criminal storyline, there is nothing visually perplexing about van Gogh's *Sunflowers*. We know exactly what it depicts (fifteen sunflowers in a simple pot), when it was painted (during one week in August 1886), and where van Gogh installed it (a guest bedroom in his house intended for the visiting artist Paul Gauguin).

Yet I have always found it mysterious, for two reasons. First, despite its fame, many people have no idea you can see this for free any day of the week – it's an absolute classic hiding in plain sight. Several of the gallery's guards have told me that visitors are often amazed when they turn the corner, happen upon it, and then ask, 'Is that the real one?' I had the same sensation upon visiting the gallery for the first time as a graduate: I tingled with excitement when I was suddenly face to face with this legendary artwork that I'd looked at for so long in a book. I couldn't understand how I was seeing this for free and without any warning.

It is also largely unknown that this work is part of a series of seven sunflower paintings that van Gogh did, so it has siblings out in the world. Four of these are in museums – one each in the Van Gogh Museum in Amsterdam, Neue Pinakothek in Munich, the

Philadelphia Museum of Art, and Sompo Museum of Art in Tokyo. Of the other two, one was destroyed in Japan during World War 2 and one – amazingly – remains in private hands, unseen publicly since 1948, when it was lent to Cleveland Art Museum. Each version is slightly different (four have blue backgrounds for instance), but I have always brought to mind the National Gallery version, as I think most people do.

This is in part because it's one of the most reproduced images of all time, so potent that *Sunflowers* has taken up real estate in our minds without many us ever really having thought about its physical location, or that there are several versions in existence. The fact that *Sunflowers* became reproduced so quickly after his death and is now a visual phenomenon in the internet age would probably have delighted van Gogh, who said, 'No result of my work would be more agreeable to me than that ordinary working men should hang such prints in their room or workplace.'

The second reason why this painting is so mysterious to me is that it is incredibly difficult to pinpoint why this particular subject – fifteen sunflowers in a pot – has had such a profound and lasting impact on the public. *Sunflowers* is not a traditionally beautiful or picturesque work. Van Gogh painted the flowers rather coarsely, and the scene is devoid of any other points of interest, such as the context of the room – there's no light coming through a window or a table and chair. It's sparse, and furthermore some of the flowers are past their best, with drooping heads. I am not trying to take anything away from the work – on the contrary, I am enthralled by it, and I have come to realise that the fact that the painting lacks fuss or ornamentation is probably a huge part of why it has such a strong appeal and can be described as timeless.

Its honest simplicity means it has not aged: the constancy of nature means that sunflowers still look like that, and the simple pot looks of a kind still hand-made today. It is not an intimidating work of art; the subject is not lofty or overblown. Sunflowers do not rate in our culture as an exquisite flower – the seeds are harvested to make a commonplace oil, they are not rare or refined, and they look ungainly when seen growing in large numbers. It was van Gogh who saw the remarkable in the everyday. He plucked out sunflowers and placed them firmly in art history, so much so that he is completely synonymous with the flower. He even wrote in a letter, 'the sunflowers are mine', and mourners clutched sunflowers to their chests at his funeral.

Sunflowers conveys a simple but important message about how the natural world can make us feel. Van Gogh selected not just his subject and composition very carefully, but also his colours. He was making a radical gesture by simplifying everything, reducing his palette, positioning the sunflowers against a yellow background and sitting in a yellow vase. The painting is a symphony of thickly painted yellow tones, some muddied with brown, some bright like a canary, others almost golden. The green stems go almost unnoticed, while the thin flash of blue (a great complementary colour to yellow) across the pot that continues on across the background creates a line we can only assume describes the surface that the vase sits upon. He uses the same beautiful bright blue to sign his name – unusually his first name, Vincent, only – on the pot.

Stop and look at that signature and the slightly shaky blue line. That's the hand of the artist, imprecise but confident. It is such a fresh, vivid image. Van Gogh painted it over 130 years ago, but looking at that signature always makes me feel like he just stepped out of the room. Later the artist Gauguin, for whom Van Gogh painted *Sunflowers*, called the paintings 'completely Vincent'.

Sunflowers is so famous that it is understandable that we may be blinded by an almost-unconscious assumption that we already know it. I really believe that the simple act of peaceful, sustained looking at it can allow us to truly feel it. Like in *Doctor Who*, we can time travel or rather, let time stand still, and allow ourselves to connect with the painting in our own individual way. Van Gogh wrote, 'I'd like to paint in such a way that . . . everyone who has eyes could understand it.' And he succeeded.

Timing

The National Gallery is free, and you don't need a pre-booked ticket to visit. If I ever tire of living and working in London, I remind myself I can dash into the gallery on my way somewhere else, pick one painting, and soak it up for ten minutes or so. I think this is the ultimate privilege of being a die-hard city dweller. Standing in front of *Sunflowers* has always had great restorative powers for me, faster and cheaper than a massage. If you want to enjoy it with fewer visitors, then go to the gallery an hour before closing and be among the last people there, standing in front of this masterpiece. The guards will move you on when they finally have to close the gallery doors.

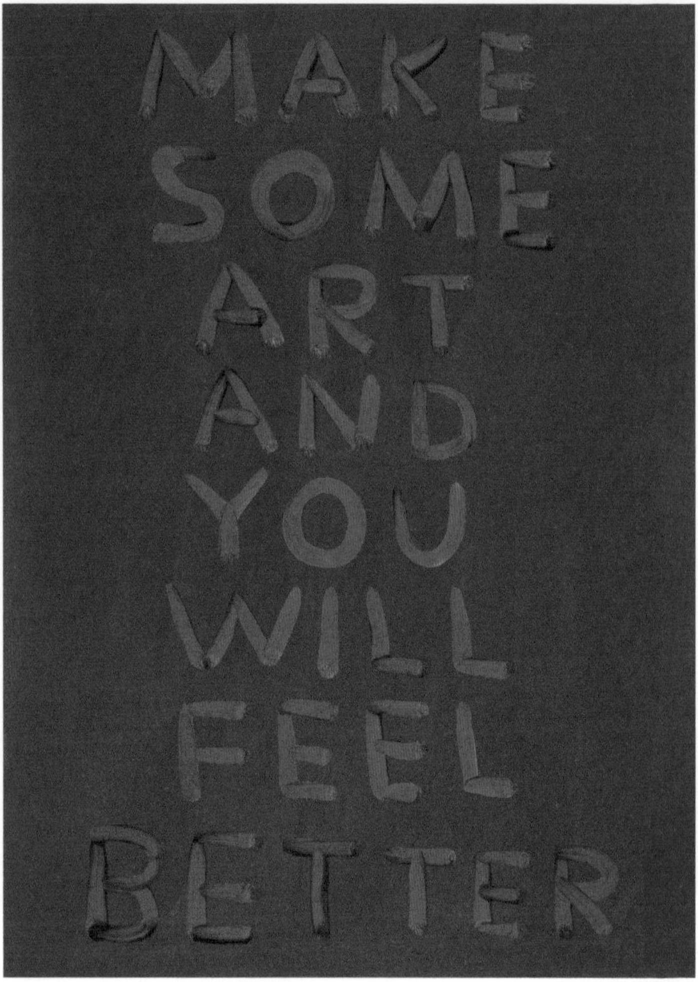
MAKE
SOME
ART
AND
YOU
WILL
FEEL
BETTER

PART THREE: WHY WE CAN ALL MAKE ART - AND WAYS TO GET STARTED

WHY MAKE ART IF YOU ARE NOT AN ARTIST

Whenever I fret that I work in an elitist industry, I remind myself that everyone made art as a child. So, whatever group I'm in, the people I'm with were mucking about with paint or crayons or felt tips at some point too, and remembering this helps me to strip away the highbrow environment I find myself in and think about how we're all connected by childhood creativity. The same is not necessarily true for every other world tainted by snobbishness, like opera or wine tasting.

We are all born with a desire to express ourselves and mark-making is one of the earliest and most consistent ways in which to do this. We make art as children not only because it's fun but also because doing so is a fundamental part of our development. Creating stuff encourages neural progression. It often employs several of the senses at once – sight, sound, touch, and even taste for little ones who stick everything in their mouths (hence the need for non-toxic paints for kids). Holding a pencil or paintbrush, ripping paper, moulding dough, cutting with scissors, pasting with glue, mixing colours, stamping, and more allow kids to let loose and joyfully play. At the same time, they are developing fine motor skills and hand–eye coordination and building dexterity in their sticky little hands.

When a child is confronted with a blank sheet of paper or a fresh ball of modeling clay, they make a decision in the face of infinite choices about what to create. This is the start of developing real problem-solving capabilities. Creating art is a vital way for them to express themselves. an outlet for their feelings that in turn helps them to understand the world around them more fully. Young kids are proud of everything they make and love to show it off; it is a natural extension of themselves, and a source of internal and external validation. I marvel at this, and wish I could go back in time and freeze that part of my brain so that it never develops a sense of self-con-sciousness about my efforts. But for most of us this is exactly what happens.

Picasso put it best when he said, 'Every child is an artist. The problem is how to remain an artist once we grow up.' We are so fearful of not being good enough or sufficiently talented that we give up. The artist Jean-Michel Basquiat, meanwhile, wanted to take himself back to a purer art-making state: 'I want to make paintings that look as if they were made by a child.' This is harder than it looks, though.

I remain what I consider to be a terrible artist in the context of my day job, but it doesn't stop my entire body from relaxing and my brain enjoying a sense of serenity when I wield my daughter's felt-tip pens with reckless abandon. You don't need to be Adele to enjoy karaoke, and you don't need to be Tiger Woods to enjoy miniature golf. Not only do we have every *right* to make art, but also we *should* make art. It is scientifically proven to make us feel and think better. I am so convinced of this that I want to break it down to convey exactly why making art is good for us, no matter how anyone else might judge the results.

MAKING ART ALLOWS YOU TO BE IN THE PRESENT

Our brains do very well when concentrating, especially when occupied by a creative physical task. For most people, this can be a very comforting way of being at peace with oneself, or in a kind of uninterrupted flow. Art therapists harness this flow state when treating patients with ADHD and other conditions that can benefit from the mind slowing down significantly. Although I'm not suggesting you'll reach a transcendental state in your first pottery class, it will help you to gently situate yourself very much in the present moment.

MAKING ART MAKES YOU A MORE CREATIVE THINKER

When you are making art, however spontaneous the process may feel, you are actually making countless tiny creative decisions. Creating art develops neural pathways by engaging new areas of the brain and marshalling the different sides to work together, thereby improving cognitive function. As we age, we need to keep our brain from stagnating. The good news is that as we get older our creative abilities do not lessen, so I have every chance (or the same chance) of becoming a successful artist well into my eighties!

MAKING ART IS CALMING

The act of making art can help to reduce anxiety and calm a stressed mind, by allowing the brain to focus solely on one activity. Researchers have shown that a forty-five-minute art session for adults can significantly reduce cortisol levels – and stress levels – in the short term.* This could have other benefits too, such as potentially reducing the risk of degenerative diseases, such as dementia. Not only does making art lessen stress, it might also actually make us happier – the brain is more likely to release dopamine during a creative session. This is the case whether you are Frida Kahlo or simply doing an adult colouring book, so dive in.

* Kaimal, G., Ray, K. and Muniz, J. (2016), 'Reduction of cortisol levels and participants' responses following art making', *Art Therapy* 33(2) 74–80.

ART IS A UNIVERSAL FORM OF COMMUNICATION

Making art can help us when we feel emotionally frustrated or misunderstood. It is a completely non-judgemental space in which to express ourselves – a canvas isn't going to accuse you of being preoccupied or self-centred. When words fail us, creating something can start to help us work through an issue. I was fascinated to learn that when a brain is damaged through injury or by degenerative diseases, the capacity to create art can be largely unhindered, even when verbal language is affected profoundly.[*]

MAKING ART MAKES YOU MORE SATISFIED AND HOPEFUL

There is a convincing theory that creating art actually makes us more hopeful.[†] Our brains are now understood to be predictive machines, always with one eye on what is going to happen in the future, even though we're not always conscious of this. Making art has no boundaries or rules – our imaginations take the lead, and we can think up *and* make something in a very short amount of time. Whether or not it's a 'successful' artwork is not the point. Your brain loves to make predictions, and in the creative

[*] Zaidel, D. W. (2014), 'Creativity, brain, and art: biological and neurological considerations', *Frontiers in Human Neuroscience* 8, 389.

[†] Kaimal, G. (2019), 'Adaptive response theory: an evolutionary framework for clinical research in art therapy', *Art Therapy* 36(4), 215–19.

act you get to think of a tree, draw a tree, and interpret it as a tree in five seconds flat, building a sense of internal satisfaction that you were successful in your act of 'predicting' a creative endeavour.

Over the past ten years, through making competitive television programmes about art, I have witnessed first-hand an enormous growth in the number of so-called 'amateur' artists. I don't like this term very much because it has a kind of judgement built in. 'Non-professional' is better, but this is also imperfect, as it implies that only 'true' artists can sell their work – and we only need to look to van Gogh to know that this is not a watertight theory (he sold only one work during his lifetime). But whatever the best terms is – perhaps it's just 'artist'? – it's a beautiful thing to see the growth in the number of people doing art. During the COVID-19 lockdowns, tens of thousands of people around the world would paint along every Sunday with Sky Arts' *Portrait Artist of the Week* – an online version of the hit competition painting show *Portrait Artist of the Year*. The weekly lockdown version saw a different celebrity sitting as a model in their own home whilst being painted live via Facebook by a former winner of the regular show. As a judge of both versions, I have met so many people who have emphasised to me how much this activity helped their mental health during the pandemic.

But making art isn't just good for us – it's a fundamental part of being human. Take it back for yourself. There is nothing to lose and everything to gain. I hope that the following chapter, which includes various introductory exercises, might inspire you to get back into making art as a form of fun and wellbeing. Your inner child will thank you.

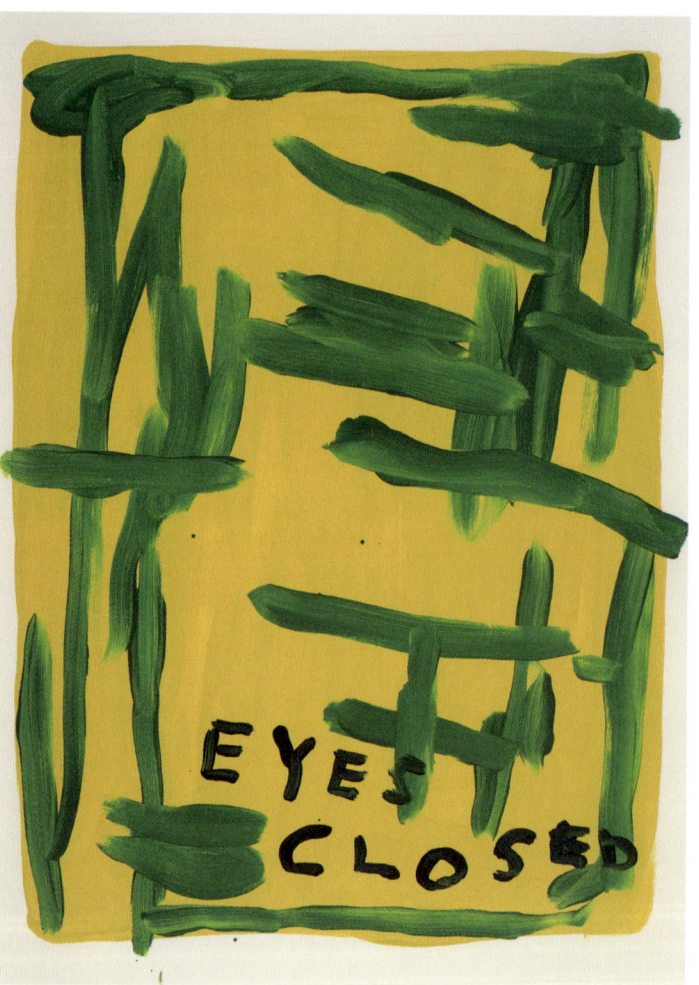

How to Start Drawing

Drawing 1 - Looking

Pick an object that means something to you: maybe a vase, or something scavenged from a beach, perhaps a plant or your favourite pair of shoes. It helps to pick something small, around the size of your hand.

Place the object in a well-lit spot and spend some time looking at it. Photograph it from various angles and look back and forth between the photos and the real thing to help you to see it more clearly. Now set a timer and spend five minutes drawing the object with a sharp pencil on a piece of paper.

Look at the drawing kindly. Don't ask yourself what doesn't work – ask yourself what *does* work. Is there a flourish? A nice curvy line? A hint of a shadow?

Drawing 2 - Feeling

Take another sheet of paper. Think about the very essence of the object you've chosen. Why did you select it? Why did you prefer it over another vase or shell or pair of shoes? Concentrate on your feelings this time, then set the timer for five minutes and draw the object again.

Compare this one with the first drawing. What are the differences between the two? Which aspects of each drawing do you prefer?

DRAWING 3 - MEMORY

Place a towel or piece of cloth over the object and turn your first two drawings over. Set the timer for five minutes. Now draw the object again from memory.

Uncover your drawings and your object. What did you remember? Compare this drawing with the first two that were made while looking at the object. Did your mind play any tricks on you? Were any of these tricks appealing?

DRAWING 4 - BLIND

Take another sheet of paper and set the timer for one minute. Close your eyes (no cheating) or put on an eye mask, then draw the object again.

Compare your blind drawing with the other three. How many overdrawn lines are there? Are any of them interesting? They may not remotely describe the object but perhaps you see something else in them.

DRAWING 5 - FOCUS

Look at all four drawings you've done. They are yours. They didn't exist half an hour ago – you put something new into the world. Forget about 'likeness', 'realism', 'proportion', 'perspective', and 'Picasso'. Look at these drawings with your kindest eyes. What can you see that interests you? Is there one small part, one large part that catches your attention? Draw that again.

Be proud; you just made some art. Your brain is very happy with you, and so am I.

HOW TO GET BETTER FASTER

I write about 'how to get your eye in' in the next section of this book (see page 185). There, I essentially take the phrase to task because oftentimes it feels as if there is an underlying sense that you have to learn 'correct' taste and the way that things are done by following others. I want to convey that it's important to listen to and respect your own instincts around art: you don't have to follow the pack and improve yourself before you have any agency. You have a natural ability to look at art, to assess how it makes you feel, and to decide if you love it and want to own it – that ability is already there. The more art you see, the more context you will come to appreciate, and the more developed your own taste could become – and potentially the deeper your enjoyment will be. You don't have to be 'educated' in art, but you do need to experience it.

The same principle is true for the phrase 'getting better, faster'. When people start making art for the first time in a long while, perhaps for the first time since they were at school, it is natural to want to ask, 'When will I get better and how can I do it faster?' I hear this so often, and I sympathise – I ask myself the same thing. But we have to remember that the word 'better' implies that art is only worth making if it is 'good'. Our ancestors had no such notions of good art and bad art, and there are many cultures in which art is freed from value judgements and is considered in and of itself a worthwhile pursuit. Imagine that at the end of every yoga session you had to watch a video of yourself back overlaid with the instructor's movement. The physical and mental benefits of the meditative practice would probably be diminished quickly – the act of comparison would kill the joy. As my yoga teacher says, 'Yoga is about the journey, not about the destination.' Try to apply the same approach to art. Your hour spent with watercolours or clay doesn't have to be compared with anyone else's.

So, with this caveat strongly in mind, what follows are some suggestions on seeking enhancement, tutorials, and feedback on your art-making.

IN-PERSON ART CLASSES

Being able to regularly attend an in-person art class will not only be motivating, but will also offer some kind of instruction. Contrary to what most people think, the majority of community-based art classes (as opposed to formal art schools) are directed at beginners. The people who have more technical proficiency are just the beginners who have been attending for longer! You may find that, in addition to learning from the teacher, you will also learn a lot from seeing what everyone else is making and how they go about it. It's also a great way of building a network of art-making friends for moral support and feedback.

Many artists run life-drawing classes as a way to supplement their income, and although the prospect of drawing a nude model may be daunting, remember that it's about the journey. There is something about this age-old class type that brings about a very sustained engagement. Perhaps it's just good old-fashioned guilt that someone has got down to their birthday suit for this, so we all ought to make an effort.

INTERNET RESOURCES

The reason why Bob Ross in the USA and Tony Hart in the UK developed such large profiles is not only because they were upbeat, encouraging, and informative art teachers on TV – the fact that they were almost the only art teachers to be broadcast probably also played a role! Thankfully, YouTube is now an incredible (and free) art-making resource with well-developed channels that take you step by step through any number of mediums, challenges, and approaches. Some of the most successful art tutorial channels to get you started are @SchaeferArt (who focuses on making art for beginners), @Watercolor-byShibasaki (a hugely popular Japanese watercolourist), @silviemahdal_art (for photo-realistic drawing), and @paintcoach (for portrait painting).

There are also various paid-for art class series available online, such as those offered by MasterClass or an increasing number of local art schools that want to make their classes accessible from home like Art Studio NY. These are only worth spending the money on if an in-person class is unavailable, or if you are already at a level of fluency that would benefit from this kind of sustained engagement.

WORKSHOPS AND RESIDENCIES

It's not just professional artists who benefit from workshops and residencies. These intense moments offer an opportunity to be immersed in art for a full day, a weekend, or even a week or longer for residencies. Workshops and residencies are most often run by professional artists as a way to supplement their income. I think they are among the most valuable ways to develop your art-making: they are fun, take you away from your regular life for a length of time, and allow you to make real-world connections with fellow art lovers. Two of the most high profile U.S. residencies (and therefore competitive to obtain) were founded in memory of major artists: The Joan Mitchell Center and the Albers Foundation Residency.

SET YOURSELF CHALLENGES

During the COVID-19 lockdowns, I witnessed some impressive feats of artistic ingenuity and resourcefulness. To combat boredom and create structure to the day, many people conjured up ongoing art projects. For some it was a one-hour daily self-portrait in pencil; for others it involved picking a new artist to emulate every Sunday and building up a mock museum of reproductions. Other people took one photograph each day to serve as a diary entry.

For all these people, art was a distinct kind of therapy, a way to ease anxiety and fatigue. The result of their consistent efforts, most of which I saw on Instagram, was a clear sense of progress. Their doubts about the validity and worth of each individual piece were silenced by the drive to make something, and their confidence clearly increased as the number of works in the series swelled. Creating these kinds of challenges for yourself will lend your art-making a purpose and a direction, as well as hopefully quietening your inner critic.

DANCE LIKE NO ONE IS WATCHING

To return to the opening part of this section, the best way to be 'better' is to focus on the act of making as opposed to how you or others may judge the outcome. I try to live by something that the American writer Ray Bradbury said: 'Self-consciousness is the enemy of all art, be it acting, writing, painting, or living itself, which is the greatest art of all.' Learning how to be less self-conscious is no easy thing, but you can certainly adopt strategies that help you tune into your creative impulses and your imagination.

Many artists play music in the studio, not simply to take away the silence but also to take them to a more creatively fertile place. In a sense, what has to happen is that you stop thinking and start making, as the painter Marc Chagall described: 'If I create from the heart, nearly everything works; if from the head, almost nothing.' This is why the British artist Maggi

Hambling starts each morning very early with a simple ink drawing on paper made with her left hand, even though she is right-handed. In a sense she is trying to get ahead of her brain kicking in, to place herself into an automatic art-making mode.

Try this or other strategies, such as playing rock music, dancing, having a glass of wine, or doing some downward-facing dog. The goal is to get out of your own head and be open to something unknown within you that may come forth. One route might be to make art with other people, so you can all share in a collective unshackling of expectations. There is more on how to go about this in the next chapter.

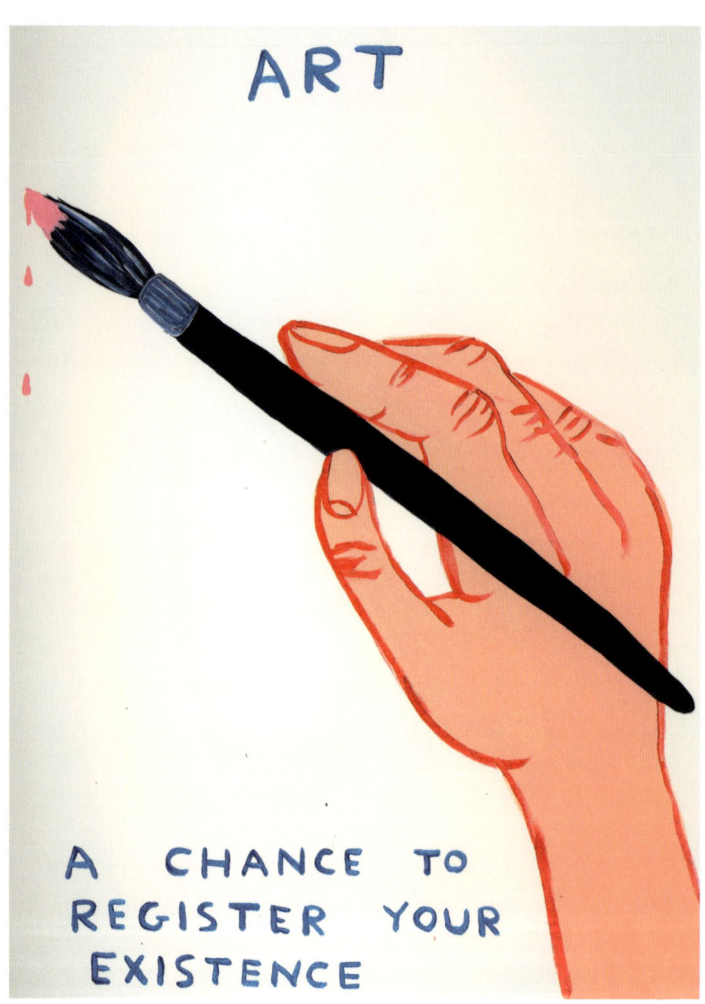

HOW TO HOST A PAINTING PARTY

Let me stress this again: you don't have to be Martha Stewart to bake a cake, you don't have to be Lady Gaga to dance at a party, and you don't need to be Caravaggio to go near a canvas. Everyone can make art, and everyone *should* make it, just for the sheer enjoyment of it. No one is expecting you to catapult into MOMA's collection. But if you allow yourself just a little bit of grace, you will find yourself in the zone of creativity, reducing stress, firing your brain cells up in a focused way, and getting some good vibes. Here is my tried-and-tested formula for hosting a painting party:

- Everyone needs a work area. Around the dinner table is fine, or take things outside with blankets with parasols like the Impressionists and be a bit of an art lush.

- While you can select any medium you like, I think it's no bad thing to start with a small canvas – say 11" x 17" size – and acrylic paint, as there is such a pleasing tactile sensation to paint going down. Make sure everyone has access to regularly changed water, which should not be confused with their wine glass or cup of tea.

- It helps to pick an artist or movement to consider together to provide a central point of focus – like at a book club. Select a work to remake in your own fashion (code for 'copy as best you can'), or simply be inspired by the style. Books, iPad images, or photocopies of the inspiration source can serve as your reference point. Here are some recommended subjects to start with:

– Pop Art
- Artists: Pauline Boty, Andy Warhol.
- Key words: flat, bold, colourful, popular culture, mass-produced imagery, sharp lines, repetition, humour.

– Impressionism
- Artists: Claude Monet, Berthe Morisot.
- Key words: loose brush marks, no strong lines, gentle, atmospheric, intangible elements like weather, steam, and heat.

– Abstract Expressionism
- Artists: Jackson Pollock, Lee Krasner.
- Key words: spontaneous, rough, drippy, splattered, blotches, restricted colour palette.

– Post-Impressionism/Expressionism
- Artists: Vincent van Gogh, Paula Modersohn-Becker.
- Key words: naïve, strong colours and forms, expressive, emotive, thick paint.

- Add snacks, music, and drinks and you have a painting party. You will need at least an hour (although, I have found that two hours is optimum to really sink into the experience without any expectation or pressure).

Once you are practised in such parties, you can go the way of *Grease* – 'The rules are, there ain't no rules' – and all make whatever you like. Don't judge your output as anything other than a symbol of time passed with friends. A ceremonial burning of all the art produced is not advised, although some might well advocate for it. Remember, participation in the painting party will have reduced your stress levels and helped your brain turn down the volume, so try to think about the making, hold back from comparison, and embrace the childlike wonder of making some art with your mates.

HOW TO IMPROVE YOUR COMPOSITION, OR HOW TO IMPROVE HOW YOU PUT STUFF TOGETHER IN YOUR ART

One of the things that sets a great artwork apart is *how* the picture is put together. Thinking about this – how you decide what to put where – is a huge gamechanger, and can elevate your artwork without any other improvement to your technique or style. That's why I want to outline ways in which to improve your composition.

More often than not, when we are new to making art, we tend to just start a drawing or painting at some random point on the page, and this is great: diving in at the deep end is better than standing on the side! But spending time thinking about how you are going to compose your piece from start to finish will have a huge impact.

A great composition is achieved by putting effort into arranging various components in a manner that appears seamless. I am nuts about the Post-Impressionist pictures of an inventive French artist, Pierre Bonnard.

He made dozens of landscapes as seen through windows, thereby allowing the domestic and natural worlds to collide. Bonnard said, 'And after drawing comes composition. A well-composed painting is half-done.' In other words, it takes work to make things look effortless, but if you can nail the composition the rest of the work will be more rewarding.

One of the simplest ways to start improving your composition is to make a set of preparatory sketches by drawing four frames on one piece of paper. Consider four different ways to depict the same subject or scene. Change the orientation from portrait to landscape and try various approaches to the same picture in very quick broad strokes – perhaps even just thirty seconds for each. Compare all four and work out which feels right to you. Although this may seem incredibly simple, it is a system used by experienced artists the world over.

Traditionally, composition is all about the picture 'hanging together' so that it is harmonious, with symmetry and a point of focus. Knowing this and practising this approach is useful, because a great way to set your work apart is to disrupt what is expected sometimes, to use compositional strategies to be more original and playful. When I am considering the applications for art competitions, I can look at over a thousand artworks in one day. One of the fastest ways that a picture can grab my attention is often not through realism or perfect paint application, but rather via an arresting composition. These paintings or drawings might have added drama, edginess, illusory space, and character all because of the vigour of the composition.

The first question to ask yourself when you want to take a picture up a notch is, what is my focus? This is connected to another question: why do I want to make this picture? Your approach to composition is one of the most important ways to convey mood, feeling, and style. Let's take as an example a good old-fashioned male nude. If you are at a life-drawing class with a life model, the subject is obvious: you are going to draw the figure in front of you. If you place that standing figure in the centre of the page with nothing else, you make it the sole focus. There is an inbuilt kind of harmony to this kind of composition – it makes sense and has a classical quality.

It's tempting to think that there is no other option in this scenario, as used as we are to seeing a traditional life drawing with a standing nude occupying the centre of an otherwise-blank page. But with the exact same subject, you could also make a more dramatic place-ment, perhaps cutting the left arm and leg off with the edge of the paper. An artist associated with the Impres-sionists, Edgar Degas, was well known for this kind of cropping. It gives the viewer the sense that something is *not* being seen, which adds a tension to the picture. It's also less expected, which develops the liveliness.

With the exact same subject and the addition of nothing else, you could do something like draw multiple versions of the male nude on one sheet of paper. Repetition can add character to the page and even bring to mind the lovely sheets covered in multiple drawings that exist from Renaissance masters like Leonardo and Michelangelo, who reused all parts of the page as paper was still a luxury for them. Those guys never intended for anyone to see their sketches, but the effect is well worth emulating – it gives such a dynamic quality to the work. If you want to go full Leonardo, add some random notes about the flying machine you'd like to develop. Or, if you prefer Michelangelo, bash out a little sonnet in the corner of the page. Jokes about your Renaissance poetry career aside, you could certainly add text – much like our friend, David Shrigley – which allows for the figure to be seen in context of a sympathetic or contrasting message.

You can take the same subject even further by giving some consideration to extending the scene. The obvious first choice would be to portray the room as it is around the model. Chairs, easels, windows, and doorways could give context. Ask yourself if they make the picture more interesting. Do they help with the intended focus? Do you want to be literal, or would you prefer to bring in your imagination? The standing figure could also be placed in a landscape, a bedroom, or simply against a wash of colour or in an abstract setting. These are just a tiny fraction of the compositional choices available to you that could completely transform the tenor of your picture.

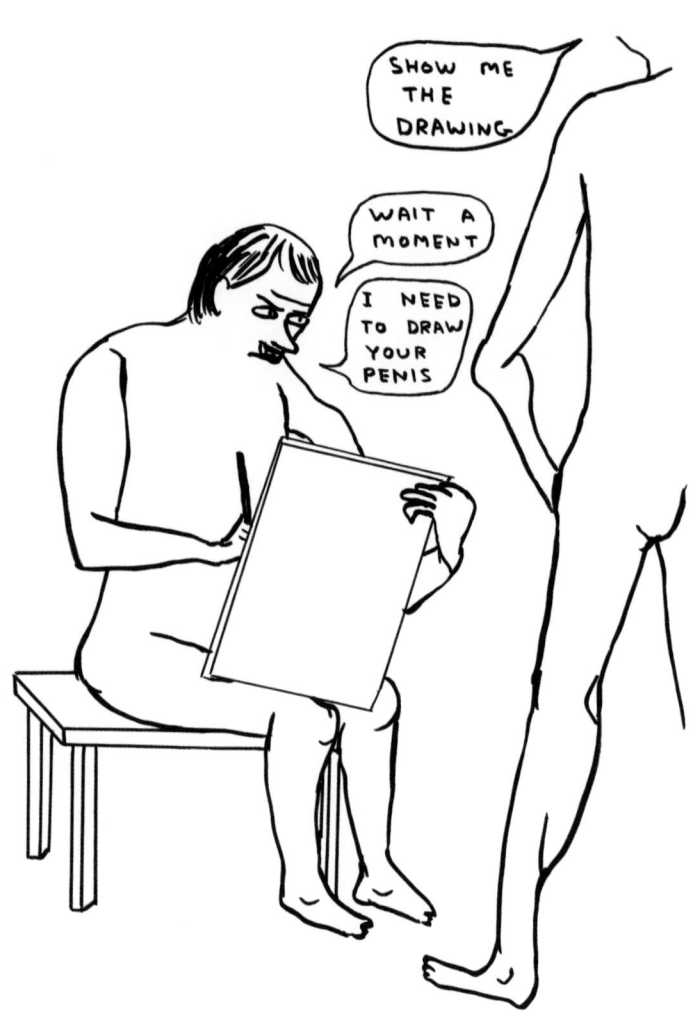

One of the greatest compositional strategies available is a relatively easy one: leave one thing – or lots of things – out. Often, what is not portrayed makes for a much more interesting artwork. It takes a certain kind of bravery to let the blank page or canvas do the talking, but it is highly effective – as in the works of British artist Jonathan Yeo, who made headlines the world over when he painted King Charles II in 2024. Although that portrait was a very complete painting in red tones, in his early works Yeo made it fashionable to leave the portrait grid (the under drawing to get proportion correct) visible to the viewer and to leave whole areas of the subject unpainted.

Another useful tool is a mirror. A mirror is like a second set of eyes: everything is there but one step removed, and in this small distance is the space to see afresh. Looking at a picture in a different way means you notice new things, like how the inclusion of certain objects is just distracting or how components should be moved for balance.

One of the most consistently used compositional devices in landscape painting is creating a visual pathway for the viewer (though to be fair, you can create such a pathway in many genres of painting, not just landscapes). This is a mechanism by which you render a scene in which there's a clear pathway for the eye, almost as if emulating how the viewer would walk through the landscape. A pathway leading from the foreground of the painting is one way to do this, but a more subtle effect can be achieved by creating an interesting entry point in the foreground – perhaps an object with a strong colour, which is then reintroduced in both the painting's middle ground and most distant spaces. In crude terms, the gently recurring colour acts almost like a pinball, bouncing around to create a pathway in the picture.

The French artist Henri Matisse employed colour differently, using it in original ways as a kind of all-over compositional glue: 'I cannot copy nature in a servile way. I am forced to interpret nature and submit it to the spirit of the picture. From the relationship I have found in all the tones there must result a living harmony of colours, a harmony analogous to that of a musical composition.' In this sense, we enjoy his pictures whether they are realistic or not, because of his understanding that colour alone can fuse the scene together.

This leads us to less literal modes of making art and the potential to throw everything up in the air, including these kinds of compositional strategies. When we are new to making art, a lot of energy is spent in the pursuit of realism – we want to make what we are drawing or painting look sort of like the thing we intend to represent. It's completely understandable, although it is by no means the only way to make art. I would actually advocate throwing yourself into abstract art by copying various masters of its style – people like Joan Mitchell,

Stanley Whitney, Hilma af Klint, Frank Bowling, Jackson Pollock, and Sonia Delaunay. By doing so, you will begin to understand in a new way that just because these pictures are non-representational doesn't mean there are not compositional forces at play.

The Russian painter Kazimir Malevich, one of the first artists to make a truly abstract work (as early as 1915), believed that removing any trace of subject matter was the way to the truest kind of composition: 'Only when the habit of one's consciousness to see in paintings bits of nature, Madonnas, and shameless nudes . . . has disappeared, shall we see a pure painting composition.' We can all learn a lot from artists like Malevich, who saluted his own 'pure' and entirely abstract work – most famously a painting that was simply a black square that nearly filled a white canvas, which might just be compositional economy at its finest!

Malevich throws us forward to the last section of this book, which is about how to be an artist. A pioneer of modern art, he was someone who had the courage of his convictions to become a full-time artist and was even buried in a coffin designed as a work of art – naturally with a black square on the lid. Now, not everyone has to be buried with their artwork, but it is certainly an intense and brilliant thing to be an artist, whatever level you're working at. Skip ahead to Part Five for some tips that can apply to all of us, and some insight into what professional artists get up to.

BLUE PAINTING

PART FOUR: TAKING FINE ART HOME

WHY BUY ART
IF YOU'RE NOT A
ROCKEFELLER

I grew up in a modest house. The walls of the bedroom I shared with my sister were plastered with Keanu Reeves posters until I bucked the trend of my background and went off to university. Like everyone I knew, we did not have any original art in our home, and it was pretty rare to encounter any in our day-to-day lives. We couldn't search for art online and the local libraries had a paltry or non-existent art-book offering.

For digital natives – people just a few years younger than me – it must be impossible to imagine a world in which images of art were so restricted. We would visit Woolworths (a now-defunct low-cost chain that sold toys, music, and stationery, among other things, and also had a wicked pick 'n' mix counter) and spend ages browsing the poster rack. I still vividly remember the sound of the plastic double-sided doors clacking into each other. My brother would fight to see a poster of a raunchy model or a Porsche Carrera, and I would push them away to find the art pictures, which always included a highly detailed and magnificently surreal Salvador Dalí. We were excited to see these large, perfect, and polished images, and I was especially hungry to see famous works of art.

Posters were a big deal in the eighties and nineties. When I was a child, our art offering at home comprised of a much-admired Monet poster (*The Poppy Field Near Argenteuil*) in a frame on the living room wall that my dad selected. I am pretty sure it was mandatory in Britain at the time to own this or something similar. My nan had Pierre-Auguste Renoir's *Luncheon of the Boating Party* by the front door, which I would gaze at while my parents said their trademark slow English goodbyes on the doorstep. As I have explained, this was as close as I would come to art while I was a child, except for one school trip to the Tate (I am old enough that there was just one in London at the time). I watched the televised opening of the Tate Modern around the time I started at Warwick University, which for me had the equivalent impact of witnessing the moon landing.

So, like most people, I know what it feels like to assume that owning art is completely out of the question. But I know that most people want to have art in their homes – this is why vast numbers still buy reproductions of famous artworks. Museums have gotten pretty sophisticated with the variety and quality of these mass-produced art prints, so now you have more choices than just reproductions of long-dead Impressionists. The fact that prints are now custom-made at major institutions such as the Met in New York is important. For a long time, the museum picked out a few easy wins, but now online and in the shop you can ask for almost anything to be created as a poster, such as works by the pioneering artist Jacob Lawrence or activist artist Faith Ringgold – both late African-American artists who were overlooked until recent times and are now bestsellers.

The other occasion when a lot of us buy art is on holiday – usually as an inexpensive souvenir of a trip. I do this too. At home I have a reproduction of a sexy Rodin drawing that my husband and I bought the weekend we got engaged in Paris from the Musée Rodin gift shop. We have also plastered our downstairs bathroom with cheap prints we buy on Italian adventures.

But what follows is about buying fine art, by which I mean things that are original, usually by living artists, and not mass produced (i.e. a limited-edition fine art print, as opposed to something that can be digitally made ad infinitum). This is the terrain that I think most people feel nervous about and excluded from, but the good news is that buying art can be as inexpensive and easy as buying a new coat.

These days I live in a terraced house in Brixton, South London. I love watching people's faces as they enter what can only be described as our own mad little museum, with about 150 artworks on the walls. It's hard to write this without seeming boastful. I am not a member of the landed gentry, and yet here I am surrounded by art that I have been able to collect gradually, thoughtfully, and mostly quite cheaply over the past decade or so. I don't think I am exceptional in this regard. Slowly but surely, more and more people with modest means are acquiring artwork for their home. I can sense a real shift, and it is something I want to do everything to encourage. It's hard to pinpoint why this is happening. Perhaps it's a consequence of overtly visual platforms like Instagram, on which we can see examples of thoughtfully designed spaces and videos showing us how to make them our own, and which enables us to follow artists directly and see what they are making. It feels like the beginning of something democratic and exciting.

Not only is it good for the art ecosystem to have a fuller audience of potential buyers, it's also positive news for society at large, because being around art is so good for us. Later I will share lots of advice on what art to buy, and how and where to buy it. But for now, I want to impart some reasons *why* you should buy art. Let me preface this with some fairly obvious caveats: I recognise there is a lot you need to spend your hard-earned money on before you buy art – shelter, underwear, cookies, a bed, etc. But when that's done, it's worth understanding what a wonderful thing art in your home can be.

ART CAN HELP FOCUS AND DISTIL THOUGHTS

Art has the ability to help us stand still, to stop us in our tracks and concentrate our attention in a digital age when we are in an almost-permanent state of sensory overload. We are constantly changing, moving, thinking, and doing. Art in your home can offer an unrivalled sense of stillness, peace, and consistency, as well as opportunity for reflection. I love it when the art in my home catches me off-guard and does something powerful in an otherwise-throwaway sliver of time, like when I pause the telly while my husband puts the kettle on. Those three minutes sitting and waiting can start to take some shape by just looking at the Romina Bassu painting we have on the wall above the fireplace. Bassu, a young artist from Rome, depicts a smartly dressed woman on her knees with limp arms and her face planted into a formal armchair. The comedically vulnerable pose signals that she's completely given up, a frustrated body that refuses to budge. The work is beautifully painted in a restricted palette of grey and peach tones, giving it the feeling that a repressed 1950s housewife has come to life from an old photo to show us how she really felt.

The Bassu painting sat there patiently all day as I whizzed around it tidying up, as I went in and out of the house, probably with an inflated sense of purpose, and as I chatted away or scrolled on my phone, eyes fixed downward. And then suddenly it was just the two of us: me and the painting. I am not just looking at something I see every day; I am connecting with the first feeling it gave me when I saw it and loved it so much that I was prepared to buy it. I am connecting also to the message of the artist – in this case about the exhaustion-inducing quality of modern life and the hilarious despair one feels as a woman who must 'have it all'. By pausing to take the work in anew, something I didn't consciously set out to do, it just suddenly caught my eye and absorbed me, and an invisible air of stillness was created. The painting offered an uncanny kind of reassurance, a conduit ultimately for connecting back to myself.

ART DEEPENS OVER TIME

Although I describe art as offering a moment of stillness, there is also an active quality to our relationship to a piece of art that we live with. Unlike encountering an artwork in a museum, acquiring a piece permanently for your home allows you to keep coming back to it. We get the chance to experience it through many moods: when we feel low, elated, guilty, rich, poor, anxious, and so on, we will feel very different things about a work. I work out at home and often fixate on a detail of a picture on the wall to get me through a gruelling moment. Many times, the artist Jenny Holzer's text-based work *Protect Me From What I Want* has helped me to have a sense of humour during a bout of burpees. But late in the evening, as I contemplate a big day tomorrow, the same work has a solemn, assuring quality to it. These artworks are not just things on the wall – they are lively messages we leave out for ourselves. This is the privilege that co-habiting with art affords us.

ART IS A CONDUIT FOR FEELINGS

Children can read art far quicker than they can read words. When my daughter was in the witching hour as a baby (i.e. crying for no apparent reason), I would sing, rock, and try to overfeed her to calm her down. Her doting grandfather, on the other hand, would take her off on his 'art tour', during which she would calm very quickly by having her nose almost touch various artworks in the living room. Art forced her to come out of herself – perhaps even helping her to expel nervous energy via the act of looking. It's well demonstrated that art makes us feel better – it even helps patients to recover faster in hospitals, which is why art charities like Paintings in Hospitals, which lends work to create person-centred care spaces, and Hospital Rooms, which commissions leading contemporary artists such as Chila Kumari Singh Burman and Rana Begum to make site-specific art to benefit patients on mental healthcare units, are so valuable. This kind of immersive art designed for unwell people offers a window away from their immediate clinical surroundings and acts as a reminder that we are all more than our bodies.

LIVING WITH ART HELPS YOU TO BUILD AND DEMONSTRATE YOUR IDENTITY

You don't need to have painted a picture to feel represented by it. The fact that you selected a piece will say something about you as a person. There is a brilliant curator called Gemma Rolls-Bentley Wilde, who wrote a book called *Queer Art*. She lives with her wife, Danielle Wilde, a poet and healthcare professional, and their two children in South London, with a collection of LGBTQIA+ artists adorning the walls, so that their queer family is represented proudly throughout their home including artworks by Jenna Gribbon, Rene Matić, Sola Olulode, Gray Wielebinski, Del LaGrace Volcano, and Jesse Darling. The artworks on the walls are a touchpoint for the ways in which they experience the world, a celebration and reinforcement of their family identity.

Their collection nicely demonstrates a broader truth: the art we select for display in our homes adds to the sense of the space being a very particular kind of sanctuary, one that responds and relates directly to the people who occupy it. Just as our clothing choices express something deep about who we each are, art is a signifier that validates us both internally and externally. But just as someone might occasionally splurge on a fancy coat, it doesn't mean that they don't also cherish a faded Levi's denim jacket. Everyone in my family knows that, for me, the latter is one of my most prized possessions, as is the small painting I bought for £50 around the same time at a mate's exhibition after university . . . which brings me to money.

ART HAS FINANCIAL VALUE

It's the elephant in the room when you care so much about the inherent goodness of art, but it is true that art can be a valuable possession. You can build a meaningful collection by sticking to $300 per work, but it is also not uncommon in the upper echelons of the art world for someone to spend a few million a year on art. The two ends of the spectrum do not need to be pitted against one another with value judgements. Buying art, irrespective of the budget, is a worthwhile and exciting endeavour, and however much you spend it's possible that the work will go up in value (although there's a good chance that it might not). I don't believe in buying art solely as a form of investment, though many people do and many of them make money.

For me (and every artist I have ever spoken to about this), the villains are those who acquire artwork and send it to a tax freeport, where it sits wrapped up and unloved for god knows how long until it is traded to another collector, usually unseen, with the piece simply transferred from one digital list to another. You can see what a freeport looks like (sort of) in the Christopher

Nolan film *Tenet*. (**Spoiler alert:** I am sure real-life freeport owners were dismayed to see a plane crash into one in such a spectacular fashion).

The investment-oriented collectors who do it best for me are those who first love and understand the art they are buying. If you take this approach on a more modest scale, even if nothing else happens, you will have acquired something to cherish. Plus, if you want to go next-level and live in a city with a robust art scene, you can put in extra effort to nurture some relationships with artists. You might meet one at an open studio or a community art exhibition. You can play an active role in championing them and supporting them in any way available to you (inviting them to a dinner at your home, talking about their work in your circle; even commenting on their new work on Instagram helps). By going the extra mile, you will actively be helping the artist have more validity and therefore perhaps increase the value of their work over time.

But even if something you buy does go up in value, which again I stress is *not* a given, you probably won't want to ever sell. I've seen it happen time and time again: someone buys something for $5,000, only for its value to increase to $20,000 within a few years, but they still refuse to sell it unless they absolutely have to. Art isn't a piece of furniture – it's a part of the family. It might be easier to relate to if you switch a painting for a car. My Uncle Derek, who was a bit of a harmless wheeler-dealer, owned an old gold Rolls-Royce. One of his jobs was as a wedding driver, but after he retired he would not even think of selling the Rolls – we used to joke he'd rather live in the car and sell the house. That's how people who have owned and adored an artwork feel. Plus, frankly, there is another argument: if the value of artwork has quadrupled quite quickly – like Banksy's artworks did in the early 2000s – it may continue to rise over generations. No one wants to be the grandfather who sold his Picasso in 1920 when today it would be worth tens of millions.

ART CAN BE A TIME CAPSULE

Beyond financial considerations, often the reason people don't want to sell their art is because it has cultural value – and, even more so, because it becomes part of who they are. My husband and I own pieces of art that are part of the tapestry of our life. They physically demonstrate the narrative of our time together and the choices we have made. Probably the best example is a painting by an Australian artist, Paul Davies, a moody night-time landscape that depicts Frank Sinatra's Palm Springs modernist home as seen from the moonlit swimming pool. It was retro, with a quiet kind of tension between the built environment and the natural setting, and we felt compelled to buy it when I hosted an exhibition of Paul's work in Hong Kong.

As young newlyweds from modest backgrounds, we did not have the financial stability to merit such an acquisition. But we fell madly in love with the painting, put it on layaway, and it has been in pride of place in five different homes we've shared. Every time we move, we put that painting up and we're home. How we feel about it goes beyond a simple sentimental value though. Inheriting an object from a grandparent, if you're lucky enough to do so, is of course special, and will have emotional value. But these sentimental objects – whether they're watches, books, framed photos – remain passive and inert to everyone else who sees them. To the rest of the world, they have no intrinsic power beyond their function. An artwork, by contrast, was created by an artist with emotional intentionality – in other words, it was never passive or empty to start with. Often friends and family stare at that Paul Davies painting lustfully. They get something out of it without ever having met him or knowing anything about this work. This is what I mean when I say that art is a language without words. I see the painting talking to people all the time. I don't want to live in a home without the picture, and hope I never have to.

Our homes should be safe and comforting spaces filled with things that mean something to us. For many of us, that is hard to achieve, but it is something we all want, and that should be available to us all. Living with art is a privilege, but it also is a fundamentally human exercise. Because of the money that knocks around at the top end of the art market, the idea of owning art can feel like it's the preserve of the super-rich. That isn't true though. Art at home is about more than having grand works on display in very large dining rooms. Look for art that is open, inviting, and meaningful to you, that can reflect and shape how you feel. Bringing art into our homes allows our relationship to, and understanding of, it to deepen and transform over time. This is why living and growing old with an artwork has a particular power that is often difficult to fully describe. It's a kind of vessel both for everything the artist wanted to communicate and in which its owner stores feelings too – a strange, loaded object in which numerous lives, values, and memories can intersect in an infinite number of ways.

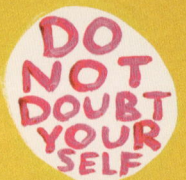

HOW TO GET YOUR EYE IN

We talk a lot in the art world about dealers, curators, or collectors 'having a good eye'. People like Peggy Guggenheim, a bohemian American art collector who plucked from obscurity Jackson Pollock, who went on to become the leader of the pack in 1950s New York. Or Jay Jopling, who took a chance on untested young British artists in the late 1980s and early 1990s, such as Tracey Emin and Damien Hirst. Or so-called uber-curator Hans Ulrich Obrist, a Swiss art-world legend who has run London's Serpentine Gallery for nearly twenty years and has curated more exhibitions and discovered more talent than I've had hot dinners.

When these people are said to have 'a good eye', it means that they have developed a sensitivity to looking at art and can spot something distinctive based on a deep understanding of a particular scene. Granted, this sounds quite vague, but it's like saying that Anna Wintour, Editor-in-Chief of *Vogue* since 1988, has a good eye for fashion. She's so well versed in this world that of course everyone trusts that she has a finely tuned barometer for not just what's good right now but also what's coming next. Over time, having a good eye in the art world means that what you have appreciated, others will too, whether that means finding and nurturing emerging artists who become critically acclaimed, or buying an artwork by an unknown who later becomes a star. So, having a good eye means that you're a tastemaker and get to say what's 'good'.

In wine terms, the equivalent is having a well-developed palette. People who have nailed this can train to become master sommeliers. I think this is a useful parallel. I once read an entire book about how someone becomes a fine wine guru (*Cork Dork* by Bianca Bosker), which largely involved personal sacrifices (like giving up coffee, toothpaste, and spicy food so as not to disrupt taste buds), intense studying as if sitting a law exam, and being fully concentrated physically and mentally on every mouthful of wine. It was an endeavour that seemed to me to be the very opposite of how I like to experience wine: in a nice glass, after a good day's work, sitting somewhere pretty, preferably in the sunshine and with loved ones. Very few of us will ever success- fully blind taste a Chablis and a Sancerre and tell them apart easily or be able to discern the vintage from one mouthful (even though I have drunk my bodyweight in wine over the years). But that doesn't matter; it's not the reason the bottles were made. I can be deeply impressed by the achievements of master sommeliers, and even occasionally take a recommendation from them, while simultaneously refusing to approach wine in such a structured way. I can allow myself to pursue the pleasure of wine on my own terms. And I know

I am not alone in this: 1.7 billion bottles of wine are drunk every year in the UK, while the USA consumes around 4.3 billion bottles of wine a year, and yet there are only 279 professionals worldwide who have ever received the title of Master Sommelier.

I draw this comparison with wine because the same logic should apply to buying art. For most people, the art of honing your taste by regularly visiting art fairs, reading art journals, attending multiple gallery private views, and so on is just not realistic or appealing. (You are incredibly welcome to do so, and I hope I have encouraged you to try everything out, but let's not make it a chore.) Ultimately, we have to free ourselves from the tyranny of 'getting it right'. For too long, we have been made to feel that we must be experts to express an opinion or buy art and that to 'get our eye in' is to be educated. But for those of us not looking to be a master art tastemaker, getting your eye in is about learning to trust your instincts around art – just as you like Chablis over Sancerre, so too can you like a documentary-style image of young people letting loose by American artist Nan Goldin over a poetic photograph of a derelict church by the British photographer Gina Soden without needing to train in photographic art for years.

The key word is 'your' – as in *your* eye. Acquiring art is a highly personal and often emotive enterprise, and one that should be savoured without fear of judgement.

I return to one of the reasons I wanted to write this book. I meet people all the time who feel they have to qualify their position on art, saying something like, 'I bought this in France. I am sure it's worth nothing – I don't know anything about art, I just really liked it.' It is a radical position to take if you are in the rarefied art world, but it's time to relax. Let's all give each other permission to accept that knowing that someone liked it was enough. In fact – just as with music – it's more than enough.

By spending a lot of time with art, whether looking at images online, walking round a gallery, or noticing sculptures in the world, and picturing yourself as the owner of these while you do – would I want that man on horseback above my fireplace? No – you can begin to build an idea of what excites you, what makes you feel good, and what you could happily live with. In my time in the art world I have become bored of wealthy collections that include all the 'right names'. I've been lucky to see collections that aren't open to the public, as well as those in, say, the Frick Collection in New York or the Serralves Museum in Porto (both favourites of mine). To my mind, the best collections are passionately assembled, esoteric, and maybe even a bit odd. Confidence here comes from doing – and doing can bring pleasure, joy, and beauty into your home, whether it's a postcard-size painting on the wall in your bathroom, a ceramic sculpture by a local artist picked up on holiday and placed on your coffee table, or a big piece for your bedroom you found at an art fair. So, when getting your eye in, remember that you don't need to remake yourself as an art historian first or bend yourself to fit in with everyone else. Instead, pay close attention to your gut. For me, the only regrettable decision would be to live in a home with no art at all.

HOW ART IS PRICED

I have described the art world as opaque on several occasions. Perhaps the area in which there is consciously the least visibility is pricing. There is arguably a good reason to keep art and commerce separate. An exhibition should be first and foremost about the art experience. Visiting a blue-chip commercial gallery (by which I mean the ones in the upper echelons) is often tantamount to seeing a museum-quality show – many of the artists exhibiting will have multiple museum outings a year as well as these shows of new work. The difference is that the new work being shown at a commercial gallery will be for sale, despite the fact there is literally no visible indication of this anywhere. It's no wonder people find it confusing to enter these spaces, silently wondering to themselves: Should I buy a ticket to see this art? (No.) Is this art for sale? (Yes.) Is it expensive? (Yes.) Will they tell me the prices? (Maybe.) Will they tell me what has sold and what hasn't? (No.) These galleries do not rely on people walking in off the street to acquire art. They have spent decades cultivating a large and growing global network of art collectors through showing at art fairs and building relationships with the world's wealthiest people. It's ironic then that we can feel so out of place walking in with no intention to buy, as our physical presence is all that is expected anyway.

The follow-up question, then, is why does *every* gallery and art space operate like this – intimidating! – even if the art they are showing is more affordable and they are in serious need of financial support through sales? For a while I ran a gallery on New Bond Street in London, an area full of designer shops and commercial art galleries – most definitely fancy. I often talked to the artists we exhibited about letting me show the prices in the gallery in a discreet way that didn't interrupt how the work looked. But many times they would tell me that they feared doing so, as it would make them look less serious.

It's understandable that everyone wants to look like White Cube (see page 27), and commendable even to take things seriously and prioritise art above all else. But looking at it from the other vantage point, given that most people feel completely excluded from such spaces and are ill equipped to have conversations around the price of art, isn't it time to break the mould? Unless I happened to be in the market for some high-end couture (fairly unlikely I'd say!), which is made to order and takes months, I'd be baffled if I visited a clothing shop, even a fancy one, either online or in person, and nothing had a price tag.

As I write this, I am conscious that I might well get blowback from some of my colleagues working in elite galleries for comparing fine art to fashion. I do feel uncomfortable about it, because we have all been made to believe that art is a separate and magical thing, but I also have to call out the inbuilt snobbery of the art world. I've found it to be a place that holds its doors closed and justifies that in part by positioning itself as a collection of people working in pursuit of something rarefied, something to be preserved, something beyond all other cultural forms. Irrespective of whether this is caused by an innate elitism or is the cause *of* that elitism, it is a world with restricted access, where whom you know and what you say goes a long way. And this is the main issue with all this cloak-and-dagger money stuff: it purposefully keeps the art world – and by extension, most art – as the preserve of wealthy, well-connected people.

Listen, I love the big-gun art collectors; I am great friends with some, and regularly work with many of them. I love them for their philanthropic support of the arts and their tremendous energy. They get such a kick out of art, and they have the means to both explore that around the world and also to acquire excellent pieces. But we need to build the audience of people acquiring art to help speed up the process of diversifying and democratising the art world. Everyone should be able to come to art, not only to visit what other people put up on the walls in museums and galleries but also, if they wish, to take an active role by acquiring what they love. I think more information is key to this democratisation, so what follow are guidelines for how art is priced.

For the most part these guidelines relate to contemporary art more than historical pieces because art that is being made now is a simpler price landscape to navigate. For historical work, there are much wider discrepancies in price: the piece could have been made in a fashionable period 100 years ago or it could be a dull copy of a master from the 1600s, and it takes real connoisseurs to price this stuff. Naturally any amounts that I specify here will date in the coming years, but the general principle of the sliding scale should remain consistent. If you are buying artists based in New York or LA, the prices will be about 20–30 per cent higher sometimes (just like a coffee can cost 30 per cent more there, so too does art). I have used paintings as the principal method for illustrating prices for the sake of simplicity, and because paintings make up most art and most art sold. Finally, some of the prices quoted here get pretty punchy. They are provided as a means to help demystify the art market. But what I'm really interested in is offering tips for first-time art buyers. Really, this is about how to get started and mostly about how to buy inexpensive art (something priced about the same as a big item of furniture as opposed to a car or even a house!).

EMERGING ARTISTS – OFTEN FOUND IN LOCAL STUDIOS AND GROUP EXHIBITIONS

There are, broadly speaking, two kinds of emerging artists. One set is slightly removed from rising through the ranks, so to speak. These artists may not live in an art centre like New York or London, and therefore are sometimes called 'local artists'. Whether by choice or not, they do not engage in many of the mechanisms of the art market – art school, art fairs, commercial galleries, and so on. Instead, they exhibit at small community venues and sell work on their Instagram. They may be art teachers and apply to open-call exhibitions in which they may get a chance to exhibit with other artists of a similar standing. They are by no means amateur: many such artists make original and arresting work. Some will know the 'rules' of the more elite art world and refuse to partake due to its perceived – and real – snobbery; others will just not be aware that it is possible to break into the art world and reach bigger audiences. I encounter this kind of artist all the time when I visit studio buildings, and I also meet them as contestants on *Sky Arts Portrait Artist of the Year* and *Sky Arts Landscape Artist of the Year*, on which I have been a judge for over a decade.

Among the prices listed below for emerging art, local artists usually sit at the lower end of the range, as their audience is smaller. I have acquired work from many of them and placed it in great collections. Unfortunately, the art world largely ignores these artists, or sometimes even groups them together with another well-recognised grouping of artists called 'outsider artists'. This label does not sit well with me. It is used to describe people who are usually uneducated in art, make it almost compulsively, and have no relationship with the conventions of the art world. Sometimes their work is discovered after their death and becomes a fetish object for collectors, such as the Chicago-based janitor Henry Darger, who spent decades making a 15,000-page artwork discovered by his landlords after his death in 1973. A great example of an outsider artist championed in their lifetime is Stephen Wright, who has opened his richly adorned South London home, which is one giant artwork called *House of Dreams*, to the public. It has been bequeathed to the National Trust, so will be kept as an art venue after the artist's death.

The fact that the art world widely uses the term 'outsider artists' is to me starkly revealing about the hierarchies and gatekeeping of the industry. There are an estimated 5 million artists globally, but 89 per cent of global turnover is generated by a mere 500 top-selling artists.* This means that the vast majority of people working as artists today are not in the 'inner sanctum' of the art world.

Sometimes these artists will get into the slipstream of the more officially recognised art world. These are the other kind of emerging artists – so called because they are considered to be destined for career advancement. The art market considers artists who are in the first ten years of their practice and/or who do not

---

* Art Price (2020), 'The Contemporary Art Market Report in 2019: The top-selling artists', www.artprice.com/artprice-reports/the-contemporary-art-market-report-2019/the-top-selling-artists.

have consistent and significant gallery representation to be emerging (for more on this term, see page 309). Emerging artists will usually be selling their work directly to the client, and therefore they retain the lion's share of the sale price after taxes and their costs. However, their prices will be low (generally not enough to live on) and their overheads could be considerable. In these early years, it is hard for them to raise their prices without any external indicators of success such as winning prizes, being included in group exhibitions, or demand for their work outstripping supply.

Given that works by emerging artists are new, condition and provenance (i.e. who has previously owned the work) don't come into play. As a result, the price will generally depend on two factors: the medium and the size. Larger work is always more expensive, which I think is a throwback to when artists were treated like artisans and paid for paintings by the square foot! Nowadays a large painting may take less time to paint than a far smaller one (for some artists, four streaks of colour is quicker to achieve than a realistic portrait), but it's standard to charge more. Generally speaking, emerging artists don't make enormous work because they don't have the resources to do so – such as large studio spaces or money to buy the materials. 'Large' for an emerging artist is likely to mean a maximum of two metres on the longest side for a painting, slightly smaller for a photograph, or the size of a small human for a sculpture – all things that can be carried about by one or two people.

The price point for this kind of work will next depend on the material. A painting is more expensive than a drawing or a photograph: you can expect to pay between $400 and $4,000 for a large unframed painting on linen or canvas. Tapestries and textile work are generally in line with the price of paintings. The price of sculpture very much depends on the medium: anything involving the outsourcing of production to a foundry (such as bronze) will be much more costly than something that the artist can make entirely themselves, such as ceramics. On average, a large ceramic work tends to be less expensive than a large painting. The price of photography will depend on the edition number, but if the artist is keeping editions low for large works (which is extremely advisable – say an edition of five with two artist's proofs; see the editions section on page 217 for more details), then the price is likely to be between $400 and $2,000 unframed.

Prices then graduate downwards when work is smaller. I would recommend to an artist starting out that they set their prices by drawing distinctions of 20 per cent between large and medium works. So, if an artist is charging $4,000 for a large painting, I would advise that they price a medium one (around one metre on the longest side) at roughly $3,200. The smaller works should be more affordable – even if they are a quarter of the size of the large, they should be about $1,000.

Drawings on paper are usually priced around 50–60 per cent less than paintings by the same artist, the implication being that they are faster or less developed than paintings or sculptures. The exception to this is for photo-realistic drawings or charcoals on paper, or if another kind of complex drawing is the principal medium. For example, Curtis Holder, who won *Sky Arts Portrait Artist of the Year* in 2020 for his multi-layered pencil drawings, sets his prices more in line with paintings, because his drawings are not a study or preparatory work for a painting but rather the main event. Finally, drawings in colour are valued more highly than monochromatic pencil works or charcoal – again because they are regarded as more complex.

MID-CAREER ARTISTS - FOUND IN GALLERIES AND AT ART FAIRS

When they are signed by a gallery, an artist's prices can almost double quite quickly to take into account the gallery's status and overheads. So, a large painting valued at $3,000 before representation might jump to $6,000. The logic is that the artist has been selected from among many (a kind of verification if you will) and that the gallery will significantly increase the number of people who see the artist's work, whether as viewers or buyers. If an artist is no longer just starting out but also not signed by a gallery, their prices also need to go up. However, this should be done sensitively so as not to alienate the client base or prospective galleries (who can't increase prices exponentially) – small increments every few years make the most sense. Just as overheads like rent and materials will increase, so too should the prices of artworks. So, for example, if an artist has been making work for more than ten years, and perhaps by now is also an established art teacher, that large $4,000 painting could now be $7,000 (not taking into account inflation).

Getting gallery representation is a major hurdle for artists and one that the majority will never clear. If they do sign with a gallery, their prices go up, but for them to see another shift in their baseline pricing they will need additional markers of success – winning prizes, appearing in museum exhibitions, having work published in books, and so on. This is why when buying an artwork, or thinking about doing so, you should be offered the artist's CV alongside the price list. This is so clients – so called because they're the ones paying, and the gallery is courting them – can check what badges of honour an artist has in order to understand the price point the gallery has set (for more on the artist's CV/bio, see page 281).

Mid-career artists are often neglected by the market: there is a tendency to fetishise youth and laud those who are long established while overlooking what comes between. Many artists talk about this period of their careers as being the most challenging and frustrating in market terms. Paradoxically, it's often creatively rewarding: they have a firmer sense of their practice and fewer external demands on their time, unlike a mega-star artist in their seventies or a new kid on the block in their twenties. Mid-career can be a good time to experiment and deepen a style as artists at this stage might not be being asked to do multiple projects and attend lots of events.

There are many artists in the upper echelons of the art market who fifteen years ago were known to a much smaller circle and were very much mid-career, such as Phyllida Barlow, Sonia Boyce, and John Akomfrah, three artists who have finally been given the recognition they deserved, and who have all represented Great Britain at the Venice Biennale (see page 39) in the past decade. Barlow was aged seventy-three when she exhibited in 2017, Sonia Boyce was sixty when she made her Venice debut in 2022, and John Akomfrah was sixty-six when he took on the challenge in 2024. The same is true of American artists Simone Leigh and Jeffrey Gibson who also represented their country at Venice, Leigh aged fifty-five in 2022 and Gibson aged fifty-one in 2024. This is part of a wider interrogation into artists historically sidelined by the art market, namely woman artists and artists of colour. All of these artists regularly sold work for less than $15,000 a few years before their ascendence and now their work is valued three or four times higher – some even ten times higher.

ESTABLISHED ARTISTS

To be an established contemporary name is to have a recognised and respected career like the American photographer Cindy Sherman, the artist who uses herself as a model to explore different fictional characters, or the British conceptual artist Michael Landy, known for questioning the value systems of art and society more widely. They will have achieved this status through a mixture of exhibitions at museums, acquisitions by these institutions, published books, winning prizes and awards, showing at major biennials, and achieving a level of international recognition, all of which might mean that more than one gallery represents their work and that they are likely to be included in overseas museum shows.

Each year, a few dozen mid-career artists will be plucked out by a mega-gallery and leave the smaller gallery they have worked with for decades. When this happens, there is usually a big shift in prices because they are showing with a gallery with a much larger and wealthier collector base and will have their work exhibited at major art fairs. They will also usually receive extensive support to mount museum exhibitions and benefit from publications on their work. In price terms, this might mean that a large painting goes from being in the $25,000–$60,000 range (depending on how long the artist has been working and the accolades they collected in mid-career) to costing well over $100,000.

A few artists become market superstars in their own lifetime, such as the Japanese artist Yayoi Kusama, known for her mirrored 'infinity rooms', or celebrated Scottish painter Peter Doig, who can command just under a million dollars for a large new painting. Is this sensible, sane, or something that everyone can rejoice in? No. But it is where the very top of the market is, so this is often where the press focus their attention. It represents a tiny fraction of art-world activity, albeit a fraction that takes the largest profits.

In recent years, some artists have gone from being 'emerging' to 'established' almost overnight. The industry calls these artists 'ultra-contemporary' or sometimes 'wet paint', to get at the unusual and rapid rise to stardom – something many of them would rather not have experienced. This might sound strange, so let me explain the market forces at play and how it can negatively impact an artist. The events unfold as follows: a young graduate from art school who shows exceptional promise is signed by a small gallery and a large work goes up from something like $5,000 to $12,000. They then have one or two very successful exhibitions at this gallery, where demand far outstrips the number of available works. They are considered to have a new and original style, and a kind of hype begins to form through word of mouth, often driven on social media and in press reviews. To protect the artist, the gallery restricts sales of their new work to certain approved people, such as established and influential collectors who can help cement the artist's position at such a tender stage in their career. The scarcity leads to some early buyers of the work selling at auction quickly, as they recognise the opportunity to make large profits selling to people who are keen to get this 'hot' artist and who will pay more for the privilege. On the surface, this might seem marvellous for the artist, but it's only really a win for the collector and the auction house. The artist receives the Artist's Resale Right on a work sold at an auction house, but as I talked about before (see page 29), this will be only a small fraction of the sale price. After a sale of this kind, when prices seem very quickly inflated for such a young artist, the gallery doubles down on protecting the artist's work, while simultaneously fending off more established galleries who would now like to represent the artist.

Inevitably larger galleries do succeed in winning the artist away, and the prices for new works move up into six figures. Because the prices are going so high at auction, anyone looking to buy a new work is vetted by the gallery – they are acquiring something they could probably sell quickly at auction or privately for at least five times the amount they just paid. This is not what the gallery or artist wants buyers to do, and it can potentially lead to the buyer being blacklisted. These dealings are all very cloak and dagger, but sometimes the lid is lifted, such as in 2010, when an American collector took the art dealer David Zwirner gallery to court, alleging that he had been blacklisted after a resale of a painting by the highly sought-after

South African artist Marlene Dumas (the motion was rejected by the court). Instead, buyers are expected to hang onto the work for a decent length of time and loan to the museum shows that the gallery is busy trying to organise – or at the very least to sell it back to the gallery for a controlled mark-up.

The prices have been elevated quickly, and the gallery knows it's crucial to now sustain them. To achieve this, they do a serious push for institutional shows, acquisitions, publications, and so on. If they don't, there is a serious risk that the price bubble will burst. The stress that this causes for a young artist can be immense, and can include potential creative block (it's a lot of pressure to rock up to the studio to paint a work that you know in some parts of the art world could be worth millions straight off the bat). Being famous and celebrated from a young age is not new – Michelangelo was in his early twenties when he took the Roman art world by storm with the *Pietà*, his astonishingly tender marble portrayal of the Madonna and the crucified Christ. The difference is that he didn't achieve crazy auction results and resales at this tender age. This is a new phenomenon of our times, when some art is being co-opted and pushed to new extremes by the super-rich.

EDITIONS - LOWER PRICES ARE BUILT INTO THE PRINCIPLE

Editions are artworks made in multiple copies (hence they are sometimes referred to as multiples). The most common format is a print on paper. There are a lot of print techniques, but the most widely known are silk-screen (which Andy Warhol made so famous) and digital inkjet prints. There are also woodblock prints, lithographs, linocuts, etchings, monoprints, and much more. You don't need to be an expert in all of these mediums – I sometimes can't tell them apart, as interesting as they are – they are just the means by which the artwork is made.

Artists make editions for a number of reasons. For many it's a way to have an accessible and lower price point. Commonly called the 'Godfather of British Pop Art', Sir Peter Blake feels strongly that he must always have an entry-level price point so that his art can be truly democratic and in keeping with the spirit of 'pop' (as in popular) art. Some artists place printing at the heart of their practice, like the British artist Rebecca Salter, who was elected as a Royal Academician print-maker in 2014 (more on the Royal Academy on page 220). Print-focused artists study the various techniques and create their own prints as their main body of work. Many established artists work with master printmakers, and this activity is an exciting and fundamental part of their practice – like the late Paula Rego, the Portuguese-British artist, who made many innovative strides forward with her prints.

Although multiples are not, by their very definition, unique, they should not be thought of as 'less than'.

I was fortunate enough to see an exhibition come together when I worked at the British Museum, which demonstrated that collecting prints of contemporary artists was a brilliant strategy for building a collection that doesn't cost a fortune and is in conversation with its time. The exhibition was dedicated to the late film critic Alexander Walker, who amassed a very special collection – which included works by Tracey Emin and Lucian Freud – with fairly modest means. Walker generously bequeathed his collection to the British Museum, so it is now brilliantly part of the public art realm. His collection had a strong connective thread – he passionately bought work on paper he loved, and which he could afford, by mostly living artists, and it ended up being museum-worthy very quickly. I loved how his collecting was at odds with the domestic space available to him: one photograph of his flat showed a work on paper by the acclaimed British sculptor Rachel Whiteread above the bathtub (a dreadful idea due to humidity's propensity to ravage paper over time; see page 246 for more on other conservation buzzkills).

Works on paper, whether editions or original drawings, are always going to be the lowest price point for established artists. Many emerging artists also make editions that can be bought for less than $300. This part of the art market has grown enormously this century, and major art fairs have sections for galleries that focus on multiples and editions.

There is a strong logic at play when pricing multiples, more so than for originals. The higher the number in the edition – i.e. the more copies of the work that are made – the lower the price. What is being valued is scarcity, and I would say anything over fifty is a high edition. When the edition sells out, the artist or gallery may sell artist's proofs (APs). These used to be reserved for museums or for the artist to keep or gift, but are also now commonly sold down the line for an increased price when the main editions have sold out. Editions by established artists usually start at $1,000, but emerging artists will keep their editions very affordable as they build their profile – even as low as $150 (for more on where to buy them, see page 217). Some artists increase the price of the editions as they sell, a strategy that works especially well for artists who know that their prints are liked and regularly sell. So, the first ten prints of the edition might cost $500, the next ten $750, the next ten $1,000, and so on. The idea persists that particular numbers in an edition have a certain value – e.g. number 1 is more valuable. This is a myth, but by all means ask for a certain number if you want. I once got edition 30 because it was a thirtieth birthday present for myself.

AUCTIONS

When we hear about the price of art in the media, it's always at the top end – for example $139 million for a Picasso in 2023, or $90 million for a Hockney in 2018. These prices are very much the exception. A lot has happened to the artist and their market before it reaches this insane buying frenzy, and the vast majority of artists will never get there. Only a small proportion of established artists will have a strong auction record, and less than 1 per cent of artists making work will ever go to auction.

That said, it is true that art is not cheap. The prices I list above, even for emerging artists, are not everyday sums of money. Hearing that a painter who doesn't have the same global fame as Picasso or Hockney is asking for an amount equivalent to the cost of a new car or a luxury watch for a two-square-metre canvas can be a bit of a shock and make owning art in your own home feel desperately out of reach. But I think it's important to bear two things in mind.

First, an artist needs to value their time and their practice. They are not mass-producing work, they have to take time to experiment, and they are placing something of themselves into every piece. I love this quote from the nineteenth-century American artist James McNeill Whistler (who brilliantly captured nocturnal scenes): 'An artist is not paid for his labour but for his vision.' Not everything they make can or will be sold, and there will be years where they might not make enough to live on. So, there are real reasons why art is not cheap related to the usual costs of modern life.

Secondly, although it is not cheap, it is still possible to acquire outstanding work for $1,000 – or even less if you know where to look (and I'm going to show you). Buying a work of art could be a gift you give for a very special birthday, something you save up for to celebrate an anniversary, something you ask for as a present, or something you spend a bonus on (if you work in that kind of place). It could be a print for $200 or a new work from a young artist for $1,000. In fact, even if you can afford more than $1,000, I really don't think anyone needs to spend more than that on their first piece. Now, let's look at how you might go about acquiring inexpensive art.

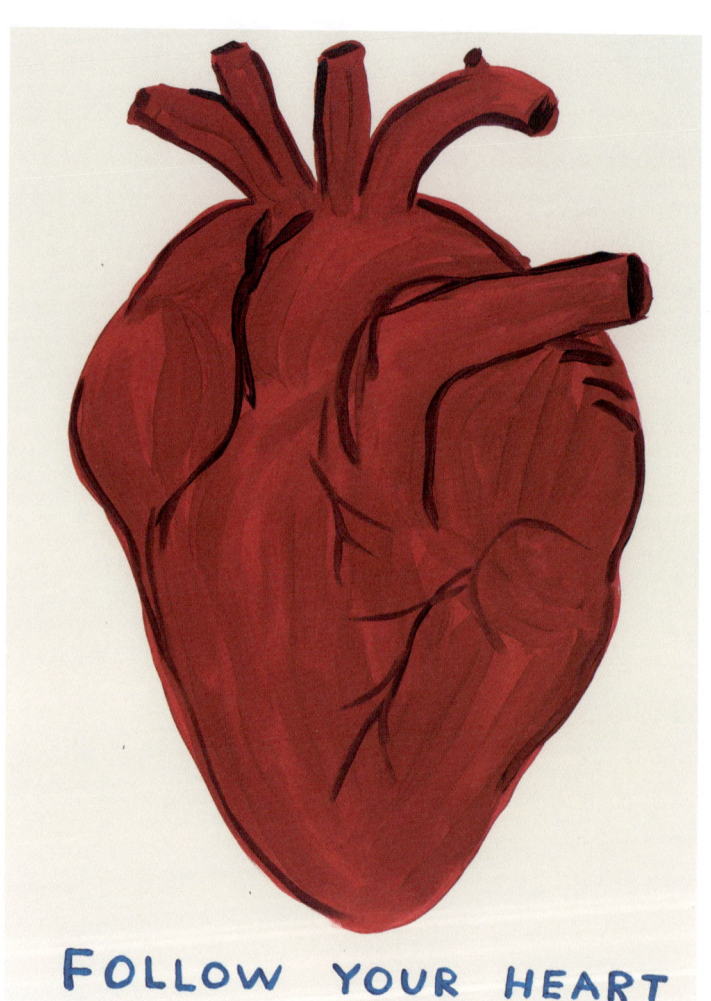

FOLLOW YOUR HEART

How to Buy Inexpensive Art

I know many major collectors (and by 'major', I mean people who have made collecting art almost a full-time occupation) who share a similar story about how they began. They bought their first work for about $1,500 in today's terms which felt like a lot to spend on art. They remember the thrilling sensation of having 'acquired' something, satisfying a desire, fulfilling a wish to be an owner of an artwork, which they thought was devastatingly beautiful or really very clever or reminded them of something they loved – something that made them feel seen, something that expressed something about their life that they couldn't put as well into words. Despite the fact that their collections grew to be vast and usually expensive in nature (collecting art can be both addictive and pricey), they always remember their first piece with affection, even if their taste or the prevailing fashions have gone in a different direction. Whatever its worth or standing today, this first work is part of their story. Collectors can defend some pretty unlikely choices for their first acquisition in an impassioned way (I once enjoyed listening to a gregarious Miami-based collector dressed in full leather show me a delicate watercolour of teaspoons), as really what's happening is that they're guarding a satisfying memory.

I know from personal experience that to most of us $1,500 is going to be a fortune to spend on anything. A much gentler – not to mention more possible – place to begin is $750 and under. There are lots of choices out there at this price point too. Whatever the cost, think about whether you really want the work, whether you like it despite the price tag suggesting that it's high quality, and whether you're really prepared to pay that much for it. Art anxiety stops many people from buying art, but it might surprise you that that same art anxiety can have another unwelcome effect: you end up buying something that's too expensive and not really what you wanted because of external pressures. In the early days, I almost fell victim to this a few times, but being poor was a great safety net.

So, I recommend remembering that it is *your* money. Feeling excluded from art can prevent us asking sensible questions: can I afford this work? Does it seem like good value for money? Do I trust the people involved in the selling? Will I still love it next year? Most people would be unlikely to commit to buying a car, a designer handbag, or a house without asking the same things, but the aura surrounding art can suggest that other people know better.

Nowadays, I am conscious not to buy art with my ears but with my heart. In my line of work, I hear a lot of people talking about 'the next art-market star' and 'great investments'. For most buyers of art, looking for a return on investment is quite an unfulfilling and uncertain way to acquire and it doesn't address the question of whether it will actually fit you and your home. When presented with an artwork I am considering acquiring for myself, I start with whether I love it. I then always ask myself if I can afford it, if it's priced at the right level for what it is (which can be deduced from how many works the artist is producing, whether they have accolades on their CV, and so on), if I could get something else I'd like even more by spending a bit extra (in which case would I prefer to wait and save), and if I have somewhere I can place it so I can enjoy it daily.

Sometimes, in fact most of the time, the artwork is the wrong size for my home, and I can't afford it. The critical thing is, you can still enjoy that work of art without owning it, unlike other luxurious, finely crafted and rare goods such as wine. No one is going to let you taste or even smell a $1,000 grand cru, and just looking at the bottle will do nothing for your senses. With art you can say, 'I loved spending time with this, but it's for someone else to own.' I remind myself that I am likely to see the artist's work again in a future exhibition or even in a museum.

Aside from the symptoms of art anxiety I have outlined, the other condition most people I encounter find themselves in is that they would love to own art – they see the value, they see themselves as someone who *ought* to own art, and might even be good or get good at picking what they like – but sadly they just have no idea where to find it. Every week I am asked where's the best place to buy a work between a few hundred dollars and a couple of thousand. There isn't a fast, simple answer – certainly not a global one anyway. There's no one-stop shop, but there are plenty of avenues that are available to you and that can be very rewarding.

OPEN STUDIOS

I have already outlined the allure of visiting an artist's studio (see page 32). But if you don't work in or inhabit the art world, it's going to be hard to get an invitation from a standing start. Thankfully, open studio weekends provide a great opportunity to visit: there is no pressure to buy, doors are literally flung open, and you can wander in and out, taking in an artist's work and then moving down the corridor to their neighbour. Open studios take place in most studio blocks once a year. The simplest way to find them is to search Google Maps for artist studio blocks near where you live. If you can get to a big city like London, Los Angeles, New York, or Paris, you will be falling over for open studio events, but they also happen in smaller cities. I remember attending the Artist Studio Company open studios in Brixton with my daughter in a sling when she was a couple of months old. It gave me a dizzying amount of art to see in one building on my doorstep and, as ever, the baby was a fantastic ice breaker. The convenience of this was like a drug, and I now make a point to go to local open studios whenever I can.

These events will be most social (and busy) on the opening night, but will be quiet on a Sunday. Pick your arrival time to suit your personality: if you want conversation and time to look at length, go when it's quiet; if you feel nervous, head over on the opening evening and join the crowd. Artists probably won't put labels on the wall, but it's completely fine to ask, 'What's the price point of these works?' Don't feel that you have to buy something: artists are keen to have an audience for their work and to get valuable feedback. Even if everyone files in, focuses on one painting above all else, and then files back out again, it demonstrates to the artist that this one work is more interesting or has stronger wall power than the rest. That is something they may find useful to know and couldn't have worked out without the visitors.

EMERGING GALLERIES

There's no hard-and-fast rule as to what constitutes an emerging gallery, but generally speaking they tend to be smaller spaces without bells and whistles located in less expensive parts of a city. They are new in the market, mostly led by youthful art dealers who do enormous amounts of work to filter what's out there and present a strong line-up of emerging talent – which means artists just entering the market rather than established names. For a long time, 'emerging talent' meant 'young artists', but thankfully that's no longer always the case. Young artists were fetishised in the 1980s and 1990s. It even became part of the way we talked about Damien Hirst, Tracey Emin, and their generation: 'Young British

Artists', a moniker some of those artists may be uncomfortable hearing as they reach their sixties.

Today there is more awareness that you can be an emerging artist late in life because it took a long time for your work to be discovered and accepted, or because you started later. I attended a beautiful dinner in Paris in 2015 for a Lebanese-American artist, Etel Adnan. She arrived late to the table in a grubby oversized mohair jumper that drowned her tiny frame, as if she had come straight from the studio. She was totally unfazed by the elegant room full of wealthy collectors and influential art-world folk. We stood as she was seated, and before we all sat back down, she looked around at us all with a knowing smirk and said, '*Where* have you all been?' – as if to say, 'I am emerging into your world but I am over ninety years old and I have been at this for seven decades.' I felt she was saying that we, in fact, were late to *her* party. Many artists 'emerge' after bringing up children, or after being sidelined due to prejudice or after teaching at prestigious art schools, like Phyllida Barlow, who became an 'overnight' art-world star in her sixties after decades of hard graft.

Emerging galleries have to take risks with the artists they select. They are picking them out and being the first to champion them, providing them with a platform and (hopefully) moral and practical support, as well as trying to sell their work. Despite all this risk, they will likely sell work in the region of $2,000–15,000 (or very rarely more than that), and are usually always fighting to meet the costs of running their space. If one of their represented artists catches a break and starts to be recognised, sought after, and included in biennials or group shows, there is a strong chance that a more established gallery will lure the artist away with the promise of a better space to show in, a bigger collector pool, and possibly a presence for their work at an art fair. It's a ruthless market, but the whole ecosystem would collapse without emerging galleries.

It makes most sense to look for an emerging gallery in your home country – and ideally in your closest city – so that you can build a relationship and avoid shipping costs, which at this price point might eat up half or all your budget. It's a good idea to attend some opening night events, sometimes known as private views (PVs), where you can meet the artist, the gallerists, and the gallery's supporters. This can be a rewarding social experience that also allows you to better understand the artist's work and the gallery's programme. Some of my favourite emerging galleries in London right now are Guts Gallery, Sid Motion, Soft Opening, Ginny on Frederick, and Union Pacific. In New York, I love the programmes and ambitions of Dinner Gallery, Hannah Traore Gallery, and JO-HS.

PRINT AND EDITIONS

When buying work by an emerging artist, you are entering fresh pastures and must exercise your judgement about what you think is strong enough to acquire.

Another direction to take, which for many people will be a very reassuring place to begin, is to buy inexpensive pieces by established artists. This is where editions come in, like a fabulous art comfort blanket. The Cristea Roberts Gallery is one of the leaders in this field and hosts beautiful exhibitions in its Pall Mall space in London. I was pleasantly surprised that during Cornelia Parker's spectacular exhibition at Tate Britain in 2022, the concurrent exhibition at Cristea Roberts had Parker editions for £1,000, which was very reasonable given her major status in the international art scene.

Jealous in London is another great edition gallery and the perfect place to learn about printmaking: the printmaking studios are located above the gallery, and it is just about the most friendly and unpretentious gallery in the world. Avant Arte is an online platform that has gained a lot of traction in recent years by releasing editions with some of the market's most desirable artists, such as Tschabalala Self. The online market for art is most established for editions and multiples – they are easy to photograph, usually affordable and simple to ship worldwide. Cahiers d'Art in Paris is a well-respected publisher and printmaker that has an illustrious history that includes working with Picasso. One of the coolest and most accessible edition galleries in the USA is New York's Printed Matter Inc, which offers fundraising editions for under $100.

MUSEUM SHOPS

The offering in museum gift shops has been radically transformed in the past twenty years, largely as a result of needing to be more resourceful in places like the UK, where the government has drastically reduced arts funding. An increasing number of institutions share their incredible relationships with leading artists, who produce artwork for sale in the shops with the proceeds helping to fund the museums. The best example in the UK is the House of Voltaire, the commercial operation of the highly respected Studio Voltaire – a small gallery, cafe, and studio complex in South London that punches above its weight in terms of both its ambitious exhibition programme that welcomes international artists and the quality and originality of the editions they sell. At their annual festive display I once bought a beautiful Lisa Brice edition for £500 which I cherish. Founded in 1901, the Whitechapel Gallery in East London, one of the first publicly funded galleries for temporary exhibitions in London, has a small space for artwork for sale by a great line up of artists.

The Tate Modern has a separate shop space called Tate Edit, which is distinct from the museum's gift shop reproduction prints. Tate Edit commissions contemporary artists to make multiples, such as their brilliant shop takeover by the feminist artist activists the Guerrilla Girls. Many of the works are by very in-demand artists and sell out quickly (and sometimes resell on

Artsy for double the price within a few months), so it's worth joining the mailing list. US institutions have been slower to develop these ventures, but one of the best is the LACMA editions shop. Commercial galleries like Gagosian and Pace also now have edition sections in some of their galleries and online.

ROYAL ACADEMY SUMMER EXHIBITION

London's Royal Academy's Summer Exhibition is the largest and longest-running open-call exhibition in the world. Anyone – really anyone, with no training or already showing in massive galleries – can send in an artwork to be considered for inclusion. From the thousands of applications they receive, the jury (composed of the Royal Academicians, a bunch of respected contemporary artists who follow in the footsteps of Sir Joshua Reynolds, the founding president of the Academy in 1768) select the works for display in the enormous and prestigious galleries. In the spirit of the earliest Summer Exhibitions, the works are installed salon-style (see page 241), and there can be hundreds of works on just one wall. Everything is for sale (marked by a small catalogue number for each work). It's amazing to see artworks by people as eminent as Tracey Emin or Cornelia Parker alongside a sweet painting of a cat priced at $200 by a relatively unknown artist. It really is quite unique.

There are plenty of people who religiously buy a work every year from the RA Summer Exhibition and pay to attend the glamorous opening night party with celebrities – which, like museum shops, raises vital funds for keeping this cultural landmark operating in an era of fierce budget cuts. It's a fun exercise to take the palm-sized chunky price catalogue and see if you have expensive taste – without fail my mum picks out something super pricey.

THE OTHER ART FAIR

Founded in 2011, the Other Art Fair set out to disrupt various art-world conventions: that galleries must represent artists, that art should be expensive, and that the experience of viewing it ought to be deadly serious. Instead, at their celebratory, thoroughly democratic fairs, artists present their own work (mostly priced between $100 and $8,000) in friendly booths and talk directly to those who buy a ticket to attend. There is often live music and even highly sought-after tattoo artists to enliven the experience. They have developed very well-attended annual editions in London, Brooklyn, Los Angeles, Sydney, Melbourne, Chicago, and Dallas. Many in the art world would avoid attending such a fair, but I know several artists who have exhibited there and have gone on to show at emerging galleries with robust programmes. However, this shouldn't matter because, as I keep saying, art is for everyone, and how much more fun it is to have lots of ways of presenting, looking at, selling, and buying art.

GRADUATE EXHIBITIONS

Every summer, usually around June, art school students around the world display their work in either undergraduate or postgraduate exhibitions. These public events are the culmination of the students' time at their respective institutions, and very often act as their first exhibitions. You can find the dates on art school websites, and you don't usually require a ticket – you can just turn up. They usually run for a week or two.

For a long time, graduate shows were attended mainly by an intimate circle composed of the teaching faculty and the artist's friends and family. But in London in the nineties, collectors like Charles Saatchi – an advertising mogul who was a media-savvy art collector – made the practice of snapping up graduate art more widespread. For a time, this was a huge boost to young artists, but just as with those collectors 'flipping' ultra-contemporary or wet paint artworks, the practice soon became frowned upon, when artists claimed Saatchi had 'dumped' their work at auction, leaving them tainted by an unsteady market that was in reality nothing to do with them.

I enjoy visiting graduate shows every summer, but they should be taken in the spirit of an adventure into the future. Many of these artists are just working out who they are and what they have to say. With practice and an open mind, you can get a lot out of visiting these shows, and your presence (and perhaps even cash) is invaluable for the fledgling artists.

ARTIST SUPPORT PLEDGE

During the pandemic, the mid-career British painter Matthew Burrows managed to achieve the impossible:

he developed a system, Artist Support Pledge, whereby artists all over the world could easily sell their art on Instagram and support one another, and whereby the public could easily find art for £200 (GBP)/€200 (EUR)/$200 (USD)/$300 (AUD)/$300 (CAD)/¥20,000 (JPY) plus postage. Every time an artist made £1,000 (or equivalent) in sales, they committed 20 per cent of that to purchasing the work of another artist using the hashtag #artistsupportpledge. The system was self-regulated by artists and quickly caught fire, with an estimated $130 million of art sales globally in four years. Described now as a movement, Burrows wanted it be something different: 'Success for ASP is when the whole of the community, regardless of worth or experience, has equal opportunity to participate and find support creatively and financially.' Simply search for the hashtag on Instagram to get involved. You can also refine results by searching for artists more local to you, such as #artistsupportpledgelondon.

BUY DIRECTLY FROM ARTISTS ONLINE

Plenty of artists now have online studio sales and stores, which means that their work can be acquired directly (although it's usually at the lower end of the artist's price point). Examples of artists selling this way include that nice bloke David Shrigley (www.shrigshop.com). We may be biased.

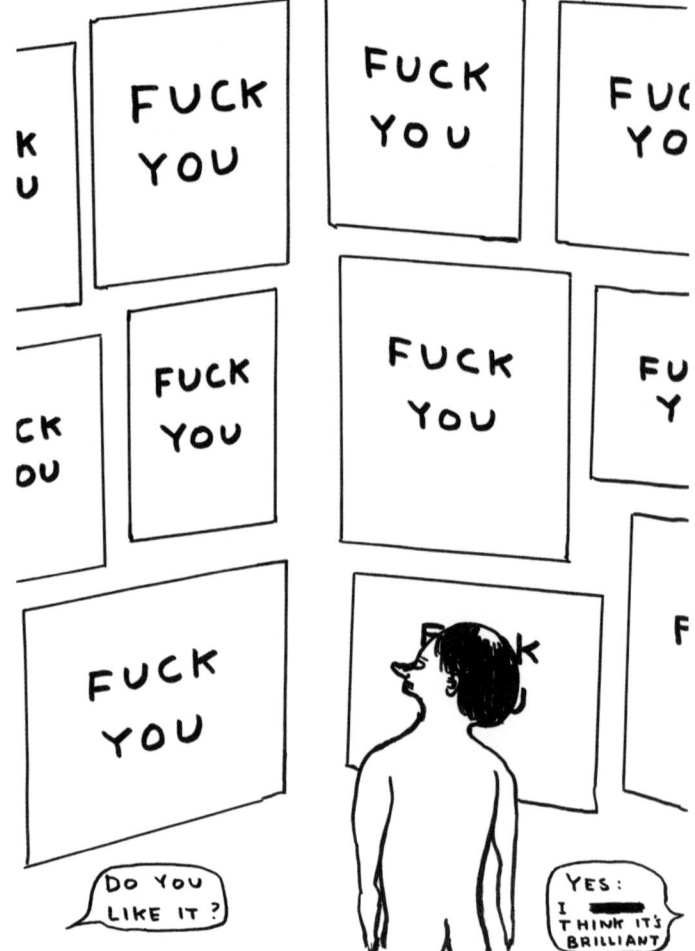

ART BUYING - NEXT LEVEL

All the places to buy art that I have recommended thus far were selected because they are low stress, welcoming, and offer inexpensive pieces. In this chapter I offer a next-level approach, focusing on how to survive a major art fair. I say 'survive' because very often I feel like art fairs are trying to do me in. Although very few people have the means to spend thousands of dollars on art, for those who do it is hard to compete with the quality, variety, and volume of art on display at a fair. Although this chapter is about buying art, it will also be useful to people who want to attend fairs as spectators, and many people do. Having attended Frieze London every year since its inception in 2003, I would guess that a maximum of 20 per cent of visitors are actually buying the art. The rest of the audience are artists, curators, museum and gallery professionals, art students, art lovers, and those who love a good day out to people-watch.

Thirty years ago, art fairs were still a closed world. They were a kind of trade fair, with a small industry-based audience who all largely knew each other, and it was rare to see artists or the public enjoying the spectacle. This is no longer the case – a development that I fully support – but it is worth remembering that galleries rely on these fairs to survive and thrive, and if we attend as visitors, we need to respect their commercial aims. If you are looking for a job, an art fair is not the place to introduce yourself to dealers. Likewise, artists, I so want you to network and get yourself out there, but asking to show your work to a dealer working on a stand is social suicide.

Whether window shopping or going with the intention to buy work, before the fair starts you need to organise your access. If you have bought work from an exhibiting gallery, you can ask them for a VIP card. The smaller the gallery, the more likely they are to automatically send you one. A VIP card will grant you access for free for the duration of the fair and – crucially, if you're looking to buy – entrance on the VIP-only day, which tends to kick off most fairs. It will also enable you to create a profile on the fair's app, which will be the place you download your ticket (usually this has a plus-one component). Apps are a recent development for fairs, and a further signal of how lifestyle-oriented they have become – maybe one day they'll merge with a dating platform, and you can find your life partner at the same time you buy a future masterpiece.

Until then, the apps are where you can find details of the fairs' VIP programmes, which tend to be announced a few weeks before the fair. These programmes feature talks at the fair itself, plus external events during the fair, which might include curator-led tours of museum shows and studio visits with in-demand artists. In places like Miami, where people are more chilled about showing off their wealth, these events can include visits to collectors' homes. If you get the chance to visit a collector's home, do not miss this opportunity – it is never disappointing. It's like being in an episode of *MTV Cribs*, and anyone who says they were only looking at the art and not the tiger rug/massive downstairs bathroom with photos of famous people/marble kitchen worktops that would look at home in the Vatican is lying. It's really not the done thing to take photos, though, for obvious reasons – the violation of privacy and extreme nosiness should be temporary and leave no trace!

A VIP card will also grant access to a fair's VIP lounge, but these lounges are rarely interesting, and the drinks have to be paid for, so they're not very VIP after all. A VIP pass will enable entry when the fair opens in the morning at 10am or 11am, but it is worth turning up around half an hour before then, because there is very often a long queue to get in. For me, this is part and parcel of the experience. It's a very glamorous queue and you can watch people palpably seething at the indignity of the experience, as after all, *they* are a VIP – who are all of these other people in front of them?

If you haven't got a contact to get a VIP pass (almost no one does, so don't fret), you can buy a ticket online in advance, which is cheaper, or on the day. Once you are inside, get a map at the entrance. If you are better prepared than me, you can download and print the map a couple of days before. If there are certain galleries that you want to visit because you know them or have read about them in advance, take the time to circle them on the map at the start of your session. This can also act as a useful memento after the visit – place a star next to the stands you want to remember.

The most established and wealthy galleries will take pole position at the entrances to the fair. The mega-gallery Gagosian tends to have the largest square footage at any art fair they exhibit at, and are always in the same location. The emerging galleries are grouped into a special section at fairs, which is usually the farthest away from the entrance. At Frieze, the emerging gallery section is called 'Focus', and at Art Basel it is called 'Nova'. The stands in this section will have a different colour code on the map. I always enjoy looking at these areas and talking to the gallerists, who have only been in business a few years – many of them will go on to great success. These galleries tend to be less intimidating as they are keen to make new contacts. Very often they will give a much more honest account of how the fair is going than the established galleries, who have cultivated a kind of politician-meets-psychoanalyst-meets-attorney vibe of speaking, where they say words but give nothing away.

Other areas of focus to look out for are the edition galleries, which are sometimes presented in one section like at Art Basel. At Frieze London, I always visit Allied Editions, which is where various not-for-profit galleries, like the Chisenhale Gallery and the Serpentine, share a booth presenting the work of in-demand contemporary artists at an entry-level price point to raise funds. I once bought a work by the pioneering punk collage artist Linder Sterling for £500 and an understated edition by the leading Korean artist Lee Ufan for not much more.

Experienced collectors will not often encounter an artist's work for the first time at the fair and then buy them on the spot. The truth is that the mega-galleries pre-sell a lot of the work that they will display at the fair – the costs to attend a fair are enormous, and they can't risk not covering them. But there are so many galleries showing art – in 2024, there were 165 galleries from forty-three countries at Frieze London and a whopping 277 galleries from thirty-four countries at Art Basel – that pre-sold work only accounts for a small proportion of what's on show.

At these established fairs, no one will have prices on the wall, and you will have to ask someone working on the stand. As much as this might feel awkward at first, try to throw your shoulders back and own the question. Remember that their job is to act as a bridge for the art they have selected.

If you do intend to buy something and find things that are within your price range, then you should sit down with the dealer – ah, a seat, glorious! – and ask them to tell you more about the artist's work. They may well have other examples at their gallery or even in the art fair cupboard. Note that if the gallery is showing from overseas and you select a work not currently at the fair you will incur shipping costs. It might seem like haggling is the sort of thing you should be doing at a market, rather than on the booth at a prestigious art fair, but it's perfectly acceptable to ask if the gallerist can 'do anything on the price' (art-world speak for, 'Can I have a discount?'). If you buy more than one work, the discount will go up but usually you can expect 10 per cent (museums and institutions will get as much as a 25 per cent discount, because the placement of the work with the institution actively helps the artist's career).

If you want to take some time to think and see more of the fair, then you can ask the gallerist to reserve something for you. Leave them your phone number and agree an amount of time that they are prepared to hold the work for you. If they get another offer, they will call you and give you first refusal. You shouldn't have to feel rushed, although there can sometimes be a bit of a frenzy at fairs. Remember that the artists are not really going anywhere, and there will be more work in the future. That said, sometimes you just have to channel your inner art diva, fall in love, pull the trigger, and salute how it feels to give in to your impulses with a glass of something cold and fizzy.

Art fairs are intense, and although they will get more familiar with practice, they won't ever stop being an endurance test (often a very worthwhile one). Just like running a marathon or having a baby, people might say afterwards, 'I'm never doing that again.' But then the prospect of another rolls around. You don't remember the exhaustion or being overwhelmed, you remember the anticipation and the thrill. Just please remember to wear comfortable shoes.

HOW TO FRAME ART

Now you have bought some art, it is time to think about how you are going to display it in your home. First, I want to demystify framing; then we will move on to hanging the works. Many people buy artworks they love – usually prints or drawings – and then carefully place them under their bed displayed to exactly nobody for ten years because they are not sure how to frame them and fear the expense.

Learning which art you love and managing to buy some is a huge win, and the framing of it shouldn't be a buzz kill. I remember the first time I went into a framing shop. It was in Hong Kong, and I had to brief the framer on what the gallery wanted for an upcoming exhibition of work by the legend that is Sir Peter Blake. I was sent because I had previously worked at the British Museum, had an undergraduate degree in Art History, and was about to receive my postgraduate degree. So, naturally my boss thought I was well equipped for what she saw as an ordinary gallery task. She was wrong. Although, yes, it was an ordinary task, no, I was not well equipped. I was useless around all these little corner samples (the corners of the frames isolated on the wall as a kind of tester), walls full of mounts in every shade of cream, and questions about 'glazing.' I knew that the opulent gold frames were not going to work with Peter's bold colour palette, but beyond that I didn't understand why an artwork should 'float' (or how it could float), and conversations about wood grain (should the texture show or not?) nearly tipped me over the edge. Twenty years later, I have framed thousands of artworks as an art dealer and curator for large collections, and I have also picked them out for myself. Here's the inside track on how to make the frame the icing on the cake – as opposed to the reason no one eats the cake.

First off, why should we frame things? Most of the time, artworks need framing for protection and to create a mechanism by which to place them on the wall. The posters I would buy from Woolworths could go up with Blu Tack, pins, or tape because it didn't matter if the integrity of the paper was compromised – if I moved on from that black and white photograph of Keanu or Salvador Dalí (I never did for either crush), the poster could be thrown away. The same is not true for fine art. Anything on paper – whether it's an edition, photograph, or drawing – needs to be framed to be displayed safely.

The reason there are so many ways to frame an artwork is because each artwork is so different. The general consensus is that the frame should be in sympathy with the artwork and not distract from it or undermine it in any way. The Peter Blake works in Hong Kong were Pop Art prints, mostly large in size. This is why they needed mounts – a cardboard edge that runs around the artwork, like an appetiser before you get to the wooden frame. The mount holds the work steady and creates a visual interlude – a space – between the artwork and the frame. Mounts tends to be used for work on paper while paintings are more likely to run right up to the frame because the canvas does not need to be held in place like delicate paper does.

Mounts are available in every colour, but the most commonly used are in the white–cream spectrum because the idea is that they should not take away anything from the work. An alternative to a mount, which effectively pins the print down, is to 'float' the paper. This is a more contemporary solution, whereby the artwork is raised on concealed pads so it appears to be floating and can therefore cast a shadow. This works well with smaller artworks – larger pieces are often too heavy to float.

Whether using a mount or floating, if the artwork is on paper, it will be glazed – i.e. behind glass – to protect the artwork. Various types are available: plastic or Perspex is used for enormous artworks or to save costs on smaller ones, while so-called 'museum glass' is higher quality and helps to reduce the distracting reflections that glazing can create. Museum glass is also UV-resistant – in other words, it is sunscreen for your artworks. This is critical if you are framing photography of any significant value – unless you're intending to display it in a windowless room or well away from direct sunlight (for more on the perils of sunlight, see page 246).

For the most part, choices about glazing come down to budget and the value of the artwork. The more creative – or overwhelming, depending on your perspective – decisions are to be made when choosing the frame. Usually, historical works are presented in traditional frames that are moulded (shapely) and perhaps gilded (with gold leaf on dark wood). This is a by-product of earlier tastes which were more opulent. In the twentieth century, frames, like a lot of modern art, became more minimal. Contemporary artwork is most often framed in simple, straight, plain frames, which are usually white or black. I much prefer frames that have an exposed wood grain, as they feel more natural and softer. For the same reason, whenever possible, I avoid black frames – I find them so heavy and 'final', and prefer the feeling of the eye flowing across a space with various artworks that look as if there is an open-ended conversation between them.

Ultimately, though, framing is very much about personal preference. Framing can have such a dramatic effect on an artwork that many established artists sell their work framed so that collectors have less say in the matter. Other artists sell work with framing specifications, meaning you're supposed to adhere to what they're talking about, and while there's nothing stopping you from ignoring these guidelines, it would be seriously frowned upon in certain circles if you were found out.

An amusing example of how framing is an indicator of the taste of the owner was an exhibition at the Tate Modern of the photography collection of Sir Elton John and David Furnish. Before the visitor entered the exhibition, there was the usual wall text to set the stage for the show, at the end of which was what I can only describe as a disclaimer to convey that 'the photography is being exhibited in the collectors' frames'. Having been round the exhibition, to my mind it was as if the Tate needed to make it clear that they had not chosen the leopard-print numbers or the ornate gold frames for modern photography. They might not have been neutral, but I loved the frames. The couple had assembled an incredibly strong collection over decades and were generous enough to share it with the public, and I felt that their occasionally flamboyant attitude to framing was an extension of the passion of the whole enterprise – as if they had welcomed these artworks into their family and dressed them in keeping with the gang.

On the opposite end of the spectrum to Elton John's frames is having no frame. There is plenty of art that does not need to be framed, including paintings. I love seeing unframed paintings hung on the wall: after centuries of confinement within gaudy, gilded straitjackets, these canvases get to exist just as they are. I made an art pilgrimage a couple of years ago to see the Claude Monet and Joan Mitchell exhibition at the Fondation Louis Vuitton in Paris. Seeing these two sublime artists – a French Impressionist and an American Abstract Expressionist – side by side felt unusual. Monet and Impressionism more generally have struggled to throw off their picture-postcard 'chocolate box' associations, while Abstract Expressionism has maintained the aura of rebelliousness that it had in the 1940s and 1950s, when artists like Mitchell and Jackson Pollock upset the establishment with their often-very-large work that prioritised process and expression above realistically depicting something. The two artists were worlds apart – Mitchell was born in 1925, a year before Monet died.

Mitchell rarely framed her modern work. The curators of the exhibition took a novel approach and unframed all the works by Monet. I can't emphasise how effective this was. Seeing the paintings exposed, complete with all the wonky nineteenth-century nails hammered into the side stretcher bars (the wooden support for the canvas) made the paintings look so fresh it was as if Monet had just stepped away from them. By showing them 'nude', as Monet would have completed them, they fast-tracked the paintings into the mid-twentieth century when Mitchell was working at the height of revolutionary abstract painting. I kept being reminded of today's media and tech CEOs leading board meetings in sneakers and jeans when their counterparts would have been in suits and brogues just twenty years ago. It was as if the gilded frames had held back the contemporary power of Monet. Furthermore, as a consequence of not being framed, many of the Monet paintings were being shown unglazed for the first time in decades, which allowed for a thrillingly intimate viewing experience (one that presumably came with a colossal insurance bill that only a private museum of enormous financial means could afford).

In this example, showing artwork unframed necessitated extra security and insurance, whereas for most of us showing artwork unframed is actually the cheapest option. I think a small painting on a salon wall (a selection of artworks hung in a group display, as I will discuss in the next chapter) will look better unframed – the raw edges can add another texture to the wall. And a very large painting will look excellent unframed especially on a wall colour that offers some contrast to the work.

When a frame is necessary – usually for protection as described above – it is not necessary to spend a fortune. Custom framing is a skilled craft and time-intensive so it won't be the cheapest route, but it will always deliver brilliant results. I think being honest with the framer about your budget is the best route: they will always be able to modify their suggestions to bring the costs down. It's also a good idea to find a framer outside of a city if you can – the one I use in my hometown is 25 per cent cheaper than most London framers.

Custom framing is not the only route, especially for smaller-scale works. Prefabricated frames have developed enormously in the past few years – probably as a result of increasing numbers of people owning art. You can also take a DHY – do half yourself – approach by making your own mount to the scale you need and then buying the wooden frame to finish the job. It's also getting a lot easier to buy vintage frames online and modify them. Often buying framed work direct from artists (such as at a studio sale or the Other Art Fair, or via Instagram) is a cost-effective solution, as the artists will already have worked hard to keep the costs of framing to a minimum and will get discount for bulk orders that you may be able to benefit from.

The main thing to remember is that the frame is an accessory and not the artwork. It's not permanent, and it's a place where you can be creative. I have selected coloured frames for certain works and mirrored backboards when I needed art and a mirror in the same space, and I have also bought some pretty kooky vintage frames online. And I am happy to admit that nestled among the many works in my house are a couple of perfectly charming frames from my local hardware store. I can always upgrade them later but I highly doubt that I will – I'm content enough with the frames, and I'm much happier that the art's on the wall than face down under the bed.

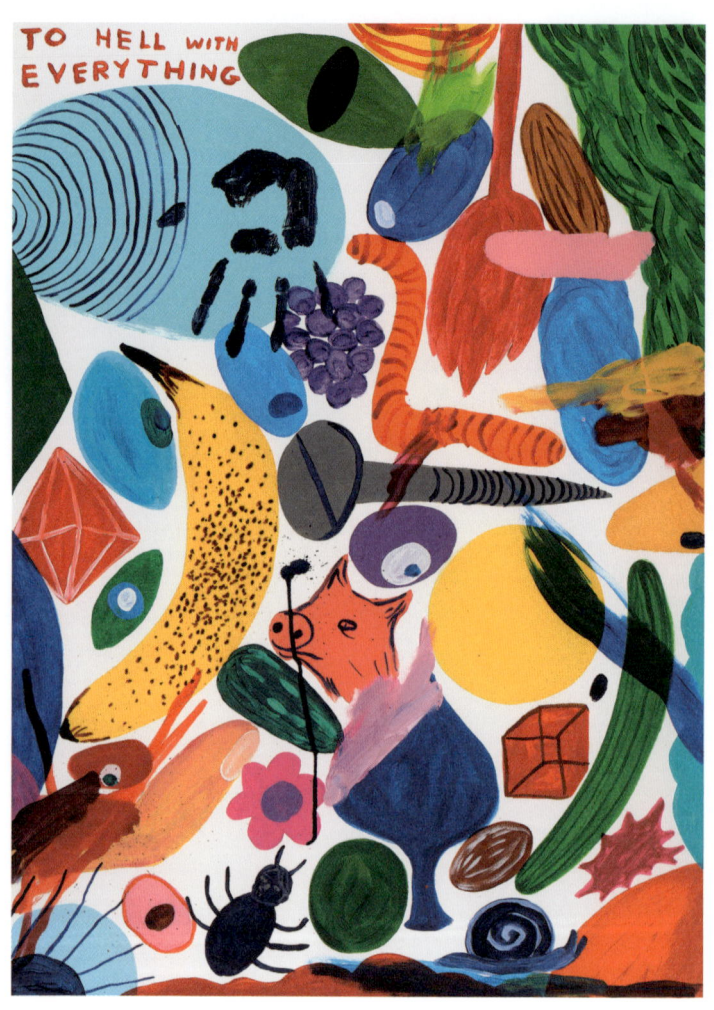

HOW TO HANG AN EPIC SALON WALL

Once you have started to amass a selection of artwork (say four pieces or more), the fun starts, and you get to think about different ways to present it. A perfectly sized work that stands proud above a fireplace or a dining table is a thing to behold, but the chances are that not all your walls will be so perfect and not all the things you acquire will be generously proportioned, and not all your homes will feature a fireplace! Cue the salon hang. A salon hang, also known as a gallery wall, is the art-world term for a collection of independent artworks hung together on one wall in a seemingly random format. It's an art tableau, a picnic-style spread of lots of lovely little bits for your wall. Like a picnic, the individual items might feel unnourishing on their own, but when they are all placed together things instantly become fuller and more enticing. Lovely things start to happen with the combinations.

The salon hang takes its name not from where you get your hair done, but from a French invention from the seventeenth century. Then, a salon was rather grand exhibition sanctioned by royalty to show off the work by students of the grand École des Beaux Arts, the home of fine arts in Paris. The aesthetic was 'more is more' – think big gold frames hung in enormous rooms in several rows, one on top of the other, until you couldn't really see much of the art any more. It was a big deal to get into the salon. The Royal Academy Summer Exhibition I discussed earlier was inspired by this idea of a big selection of art, but without the restrictions on who could be included. How the Royal Academy hangs the artworks across a wall – a bit higgledy-piggledy and with a mix of size and shapes and colours – is a good place to seek for inspiration for your own version.

In the second half of the twentieth century, minimalist design reigned supreme. It was not considered chic to hang so many works together, so for a while the pre-vailing trend was for white box galleries with sparse installation – the more sparse, the more refined. But the salon hang didn't disappear altogether. Some galleries kept it, and it became an inspiration for people's homes, where it either signified something vintage-styled (if the works were historical or sported epic gold frames) or quirky and fun (if it was a jumble of more modern things).

When created in domestic spaces, a salon hang quickly elevates the art offering. Aside from signifying that you have taken the time and energy to curate the works, they are a great way to show lots of artworks in a small space. They can also be cost-effective – you can slip in some really inexpensive things and still have a wall that bursts with energy and screams, 'LOOK! ART!' The thought of getting going with a salon hang can be painful, like me when confronted with lighting a BBQ – I know the key components, but just not the right order or approach. I can't help you with the sausages, but I can shed some light on how to think about and design your dream salon hang.

When well executed, a salon hang creates visual surprises and unusual juxtapositions, but without a bit of consideration it can seem crowded or wonky (although, as I will explain, I believe there is such a thing as wonky in a good way). Ironically, the best salon walls work so well because a lot of thought went into making them look totally organic. Where to begin? Select a wall with natural daylight if you can, and one with either generous height or width. It won't be very easy to create a salon wall on the smallest wall in the room or the narrow slice outside your bedroom that can only fit three pictures. The larger wall in the living room, the wall above your bed, or stairways are all good starting points. The more space and the more work, the greater the overall impression will be.

If you plan to add extra works over time, start in the middle of the available wall space and let the selection emerge slowly from there. If you already have a large enough number for the space, then find the biggest works and spread them out evenly – perhaps one at each end and one in the middle (if you only have one larger piece, then in the middle is always best). Think of these as your anchor points. Fill in the gaps with smaller works. A key consideration is to make sure that the edges of the frames do not line up either horizontally or vertically – they should always be slightly 'off' to make the whole thing feel spontaneous and not geometric (aka wonky in a good way). You are trying to create a kind of flow, though, so the pathways between works shouldn't be blocked off – they should be like a gentle maze.

Colour placement also comes into play. The whole effect should be balanced, so if there are two much bolder works, split them up. Also separate similar works such as landscapes, text-based works, or things by the same artist. You want to avoid the eye settling on one area only. Different coloured frames work well – if they are all white the whole thing starts to look a bit clinical, and if they're all black the walls will feel too heavy. Mix in some wood tones, grey, ash, gold, and even coloured frames if they are appealing to you and they work with the art. It's also advantageous to add some irregular shapes or sizes to give the wall more energy, such as a painted plate, unframed textile work, wall-based sculptures (or small pieces on shelves or in a Perspex box), tiny paintings on unusual surfaces like glass or metal, or, my favourite, tondos (art speak for circular paintings).

If you want maximum effect on minimum budget (me too), then mix in framed museum postcards, kid's artwork, and charity-shop finds that you love with the 'big guns'. The wall is a reflection of your varied tastes and spending power, just like your wardrobe or pantry. It is incredibly rare, even for the mega-rich, to own all designer clothing; there's always some basic t-shirts or ordinary gym wear in the wardrobe, just as top chefs still eat baked beans or hot dogs. Art shouldn't be any different.

A top tip to save banging nails into your walls before you know you have it right: put a white sheet on the floor (ideally in front of the wall you plan to hang on), then arrange the works on the sheet and keep playing until you feel it's getting there. Stand on a chair and take a photo on your phone from above. Now hold your phone up to the wall. How does the hang look in the space? Does anything stick out? If it seems squished, or repetitive, or if anything looks lonely, rethink it.

Finally, a dirty secret: just as I refuse to wash my hair if I am not leaving the house, I refuse to put extra holes in the wall if I want to swap out a similar-sized artwork. Sometimes breaking your own rules and just putting something where it *can* go without getting the hammer or drill out makes for a perfectly good placement. Yes, it *should* be an inch to the right, but maybe you are ahead of the pack? Maybe that slightly larger gap is incredibly chic? This is art, and – let me say it one more time – all the rules are mere illusion.

How to Look After Art

I understand why people, myself included, don't like to refer to themselves as 'art collectors'. It's too grand a term. Despite this natural resistance to a phrase that feels elitist, there is something everyone who owns any amount of art (of any kind) should be doing, and that's caring for it in the long term. Place a Polaroid in a sunny spot and say goodbye to it before your next car payment is due. Not everything is an accident waiting to happen, but there are simple ground rules to follow that will pay dividends as art lives on past its maker.

Handle with Care

Take your time when handling art of any kind. Wash your hands first. If something is white or pale in colour, wearing gloves is important to prevent finger marks. Don't over-burden yourself when moving lots of art around. I once nearly had a heart attack when I saw a friend holding framed artworks under her armpits and two more in her hands.

Positioning

Polaroids, photograms, and cyanotypes (the latter made on special paper that reacts to UV light without a camera) are all extremely sensitive to daylight because of the way in which they are made. They are absolutely worth acquiring, but don't place them in direct sunlight or even in a sunny room. More mainstream photography (whether film or digital) is also light-sensitive and shouldn't be placed in direct sunlight. You can preserve the condition of your photographic work in the long term by paying extra for UV-resistant glazing. It might hurt a bit at the time, but, like going to the dentist, you know it's money you will be pleased you spent later. Collages made from found materials like newspapers or magazines will have been cheaply printed on paper not made to last, so these should also be UV-protected and displayed in the shade only.

Paintings that are unglazed should be kept at least a foot above anywhere people will sit so that no one leans their head back on the work. Oil paintings will be unhappy above a radiator or a working fireplace due to the heat fluctuations. Acrylic paint is more stable and hardier in the long run. Sculptures should be placed where they cannot be knocked. A nearby slamming door can unsettle a ceramic work in small increments every day until eventually it nosedives to the floor.

Works on paper will literally wilt in the frame in a humid environment. I sadly witnessed an ink on Japanese rice paper grow some nasty mould in Hong Kong. This is why it's ill advised to display artworks in your bathroom. Even if you have humidity regulators in your home and plenty of bathroom ventilation, the damp monsters will still come for your art, so I stick to industrial materials or ceramics on the bathroom wall.

CLEANING

The best rule for cleaning is to avoid chemicals at all costs. Do the least invasive maintenance possible. For framed works, a clean damp cloth on the frame will remove dust. For the glass a clean untreated dust cloth should be sufficient, but if there are marks to remove use simple washing-up liquid on a clean damp cloth, then dry gently with a paper towel, rubbing in a circular motion to avoid smears. If you get a small nick in a frame, you can usually cover it up with a marker of a suitable colour (please don't judge me, but I do this all the time). For anything more serious, the framer can sort it for you with minimal cost and fuss. An old-fashioned feather duster is brilliant for sculptures and canvases alike. If there is anything sinister that needs to be removed from an artwork's surface (I've dealt with baby food, a dead fly, and a coffee splash) then stop and think. Don't go anywhere near it until you have a sensible plan. Master conservators will tell you there is a solution for everything, and often the most difficult things to reverse are those done in a panic to 'fix' the problem.

STORING

Store artwork carefully. Unframed works are much better flat against a hard surface than in a tube to avoid ridges forming. Framed works should be bubble-wrapped, with foam corners ideally. Unframed canvases should still be bubble-wrapped. It makes a lot of sense to label artworks in storage – e.g. if you're moving house – to avoid opening them unnecessarily.

CATALOGUING

If I could go back in time fifteen years, I wouldn't buy Bitcoin, I would start my art inventory back when I only owned a few things. This is an unbelievably useful collection of data that is very simple to do as you start and much harder work to retroactively complete. I use Airtable, a free software that works well for visual people like me, but many people use a simple Excel spreadsheet. You should include the artist's name, an image of the artwork (including the back of the work if it's signed on the reverse), an image of the certificate of authenticity and/or the invoice if you have one, the year the work was made, the medium (what it's made of), the edition number if it's a multiple, the size of the work, whether it's framed (and if so the framed size), the price on acquisition, where it was acquired, the seller's contact details, a link to the artist's website or Instagram, and where the work is currently located.

Even if you own five artworks, it's worth creating a catalogue and paying attention to the light and heat levels in your home. It may not be Versailles, but looking after your art in small ways now will make your life easier in the long run. And who knows: your small efforts may even benefit future generations, when it turns out the painting you bought at a graduate art show for a few hundred dollars is now worth thousands and feels like a part of the family.

PART FIVE :
EVERYONE CAN ART
BUT SOME OF US
CAN BE ARTISTS

WHY BE AN ARTIST (WITH ADVICE FROM DAVID SHRIGLEY)

There are more artists working today than at any other point in human history. There is a myriad of interconnecting reasons for this, from greater access to healthcare and education to the fact that we live in a highly visual age, we share a deeply interconnected world via extraordinary digital and physical advancements, and culture is highly prized. The sheer number of artists might seem like a reason to *not* pursue such a life as a career, for the competition is so fierce.

However, something I have come to understand over the course of my life so far is that, for many people, being an artist isn't much of a choice. The act of making art is an essential part of what they do – it is, in many ways, their *way* of being alive, a kind of survival strategy. Being an artist is a logical, if daunting, extension of this. What's exciting to me as someone who is most certainly *not* an artist, but who spends a lot of time with artists, is not only that we benefit from such creative souls walking the planet because they dedicate their time to the pursuit of something that transcends simple explanation and communicates on a profound level, but also that, if we tune in, we can learn an awful lot from them. So, although this part of the book is primarily designed to serve aspiring or existing artists, it might help us all to lead more creative lives and to be sensitive to the world around us in new ways.

Being an artist isn't about how you hold your paintbrush, expose your photograph, or assemble textiles. It's more about *why* you want to do those things, about the need to make an impulse, desire, fascination, obsession, or feeling tangible – it's a question about expression beyond language. As the fabulous Surrealist artist René Magritte put it, 'Art evokes the mystery without which the world would not exist.' The reason you want to make art is likely to be indefinable – there will not be a single answer, and it will shift moment to moment, year upon year.

Nearly all artists have to face on a semi-regular basis a kind of existential crisis, which might express itself as 'Why am I doing this?', 'What do I hope is going to happen?', 'What is the point of this?', 'Where am I going?', 'Is anybody going to care?' As much as we might wish for a simple solution that explained all those anxieties away, the fact is that these questions are a form of searching, and artists are fundamentally explorers and seekers of meaning. Perhaps the thing that separates those of us viewing art and making it for fun and the ones reading this who call themselves artists, is that the latter have stepped into a different realm and given themselves over to something that they cannot ever fully understand, explain, master or be entirely at peace with. To dedicate yourself to being an artist is to reckon with the unknown. As Georgia O'Keeffe said so encouragingly, 'Whether you succeed or not is irrelevant – there is no such thing. Making your unknown known is the important thing.'

Being an artist allows you both the pleasure and the pain of living in this unsettled terrain. The pursuit of creating a work of art is often described as a nebulous journey, on which the idea or the end point keeps slipping out of reach and shape-shifting to something new and unexpected. I love how Francis Bacon describes this feeling: 'I don't in fact know very often what the paint will do, and it does many things which are very much better than I could make it do.' The notion of a perfect work of art is a misnomer, an impossibility, and making some kind of peace with that while simultaneously working towards it is something that I think all of us can relate to. The idea that we can perfect or control our lives is something of an illusion but where would we be without trying?

Ultimately, artists have to harness the unexpected, embrace failure, and make constant new beginnings. And then something remarkable happens, which is that they step away from their art and it has a whole other life without them. There is a specific facial expression that I don't get to see often, but when I do, I always attempt to remember it – it occurs when an artist sees something they made successfully existing in the world. It's a precious thing to witness; us non-artists can only imagine the sensation of that particular kind of uncanny satisfaction.

There are many artists who have lodged their way of seeing the world into my brain, who have expressed something that feels so right to me that I have absorbed it into my being. On a simple level, I love van Gogh and I cannot look at any real or depicted sunflower without feeling his work. Likewise, every time I see a large flock of birds, I always bring to mind a pioneering work by the Dutch duo Drift, who staged a performance called *Franchise Freedom* in Miami in 2017. An autonomously flying swarm of lit-up drones against the night sky was created using data collected over years of studying groups of flying starlings. By harnessing what nature does so effortlessly into technology, the piece left everyone awestruck. The art was a bridge back to seeing the poetry of the natural world, a gift from Drift and their collaborators to those assembled on the beach below. The sharpness of their idea and the beauty of its execution mean that I have marvelled at the patterns of soaring, swooping birds every time I have seen them since.

In both of these examples, the artworks left such a strong impression that they reminded me to look anew at the world. It's too easy to look at things habitually, and that means we can switch off to the sublime in the everyday. Artists remind us to keep looking and marvelling at the beauty around us.

Creating something that connects is incredibly satisfying, but it is not a given, and artists have to be disciplined to keep making work even in the face of great doubt about whether they will ever achieve adulation and reward. It is one of the greatest double-edged swords of being an artist. How brilliant to have no boss, no imposed schedule, no restrictions, no orders, and yet this independence can bring with it aspects that are less appealing: isolation, self-doubt, sporadic income, creative block, and a sense of the unknown. Practising artists decide the trade-off is worth it, and thank goodness they do. As a token of my gratitude, the remainder of this section contains insights I have gleaned from the artists I've encountered into how to overcome, or at least live with, the less desirable aspects of being an artist, as well as some practical considerations that they don't teach at art school – like how to actually make some money and how to stay motivated.

But first, here's some advice from an artist himself: David Shrigley.

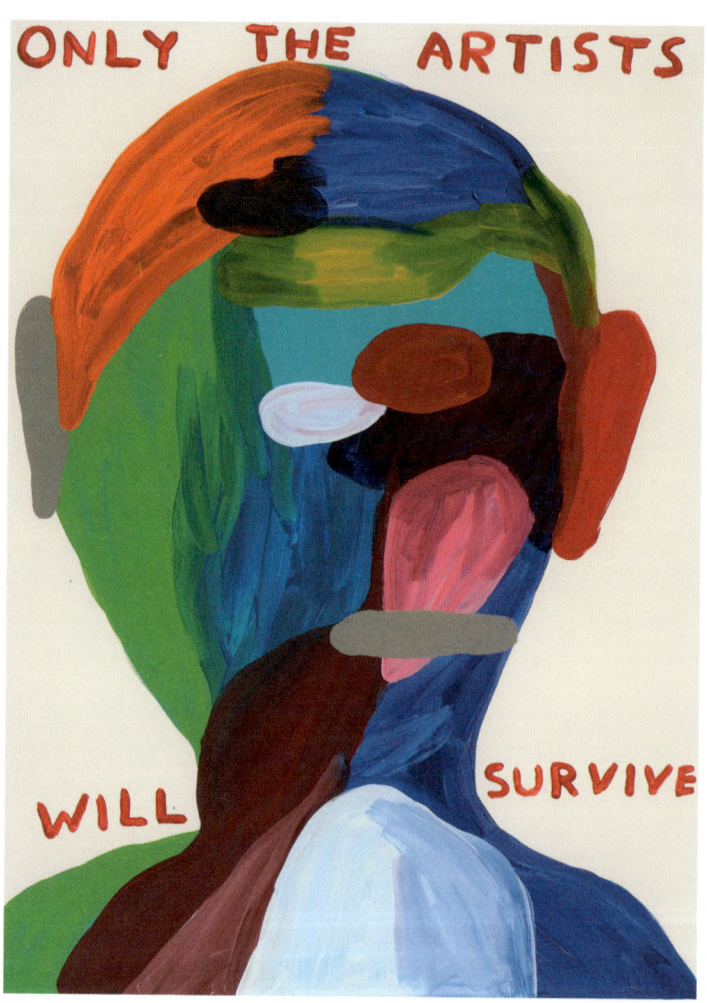

GUIDANCE FROM DAVID SHRIGLEY

My thoughts about art

Art is not a demonstration of excellence. Art is an enquiry: a process to discover things.

I try to treat every day in the studio as if it is my first: I always want to be at the beginning; for everything to be new.

Making art makes me happy. It is a form of therapy.

Craft is important, but it is a different thing to art. Craft skills are very helpful, but it is possible to make art without them. You can learn craft skills if you need them, or you can get someone more talented to help you.

If you are not an artist but would like to be one, then all you need to do is make some art; then you will be an artist. You don't need to have studied art or be able to draw or have a studio. You can make art anytime, anywhere, and with anything. Sometimes you can make art with nothing.

Advice for the artist

Allot time to make art and make the art whether you feel like it or not. If you put the hours in, then the art makes itself.

Try to discover something new every day.

The way you feel about what you have made will change. Avoid discarding the works that you don't like. You are likely to change your opinion of them at a later date.

The most important opinion is your own. Don't worry about what other people think. Listen to advice but bear in mind it might be wrong.

The ideal mix for the artist's ego is:

- one part humility

- one part self-confidence

- one part self-delusion.

If you're tired, take a nap.

Moderate use of caffeine and sugar might help you to make art, but alcohol and drugs will not.

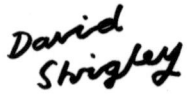

HOW TO FIND
YOUR STYLE

Before you can hope to sell your work, you need to make something that you can stand by, and you need to know who you are as an artist. For many artists, this might involve finding your style. This is obvious, but it really bears repeating: there is no one way to be an artist and there is no one way to make artwork. I meet so many aspiring artists who struggle with this fundamental issue, which prohibits them from developing and accepting their own style. They can't yet value what they in particular are seeing, thinking, and making. They want to be like someone else, not just because they like that style but because that artist has been validated and 'accepted'.

But it's vital to remember that the artist you so admire was not validated at first – they were original and owned their own space, and then their unique way of working came to be recognised later. Your style, or rather the small things that make your work yours – such as the subjects you select, the way you translate them, and the process you devise – all need to be sensitively and carefully shaped and treated like precious assets.

I remember mentoring the British artist Gommie a few years ago, who lamented, 'I just don't think I am the right kind of artist, if I am an artist at all. No one else would make work like this.' I laughed, because he saw this as a negative and I had selected him to work with precisely because of this difference. He hasn't been to art school; instead he was a trained actor and had given up the stage in pursuit of something that allowed him to be more in charge of his creative impulses. Just after the Brexit vote, he set off with a set of large fold-out Ordnance Survey maps and a tent on various long walks across the UK. While walking, he would meet locals and capture pertinent sentiments they shared in short poems. He then decided to paint the maps and include the small snippets of poems on top. He didn't always think these painted poems were 'a thing', and would often dismiss the idea he was making paintings at all.

My job was to tell him that the part he was most nervous about, the part that didn't seem 'right' or 'the done thing' was the part to most proudly own. He is now known as the poet-artist Gommie, and his paintings, since he has allowed them to be referred to as such, have gone from strength to strength. There will always be doubt – it's completely natural to second-guess yourself in the act of creativity – but you have to pay no attention to negative thoughts that diminish or sideline what makes you *you*.

Therefore, when it comes to finding your style, the key thing is to experiment and play. It doesn't have to be 'good', it just has to be made. Returning again and again to the act of making art is the thing that will make you an artist. Some artists say that the style finds them. Gustave Flaubert, the author of *Madame Bovary*, said the opposite, and although he was talking about writing, I think it is important to keep in mind: 'One arrives at style only with atrocious effort, with fanatical and devoted stubbornness.' Style is something you will have to put time into and that will come to be like an extension of your personality in 2D or 3D form. As it is an expression of your feelings, experience, and knowledge, it is also likely to change over time, either by major force on your own part or with subtle shifts over the years.

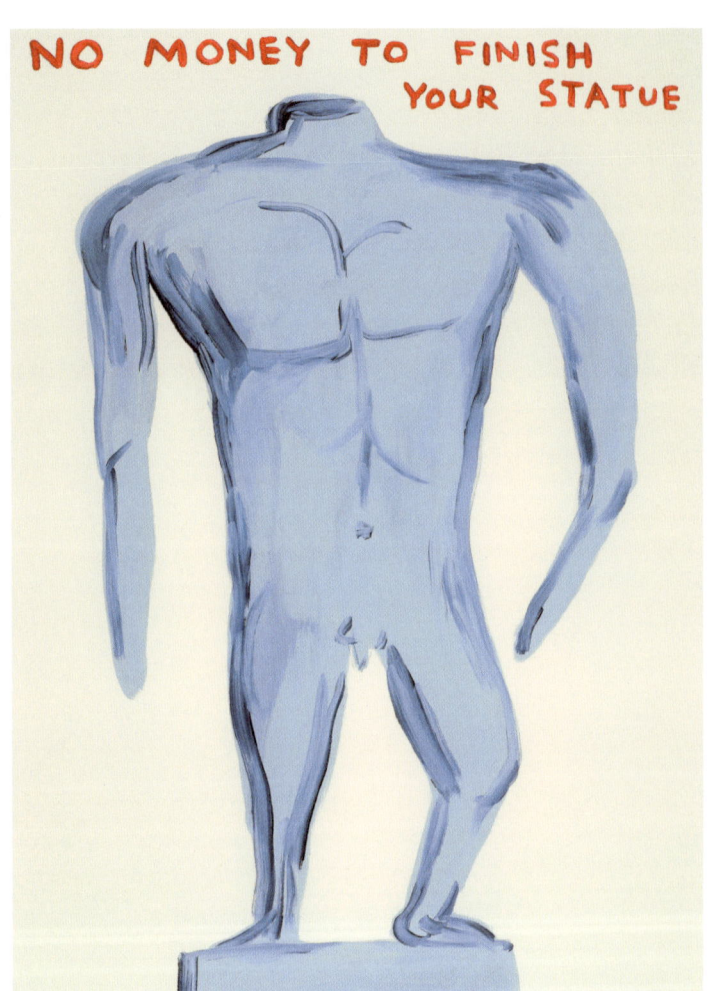

HOW TO MAKE A LIVING AS AN ARTIST

Most artists I have met do not like talking about money. Lubaina Himid, a brilliant British artist, told me once she'd rather talk about sex! She is not unique in this regard. Back in the 1800s, the French artist Gustave Courbet wrote, 'You will have noticed that I have not said a word about the price . . . all artists, myself in particular, loathe these discussions of numbers.' For a long time, the idea of selling one's work has been equated with 'selling out', and to be visibly interested in cultivating your own market was seen as so perverse that it surely meant the art could not be serious.

Andy Warhol famously broke these taboos by writing and talking about the business of art, even saying, 'Making money is art and working is art and good business is the best art.' But the attitude that selling art is vulgar remains a hangover from the romantic notion of the artist as a tortured soul that took centre stage in the nineteenth century – an isolated figure who drank and smoked too much in their damp garret and was lauded as a genius only after their death. We have to remain alert to this misleading narrative, and in fact many artists throughout history were quietly very astute businesspeople – those running the most successful Renaissance workshops would give today's business- and brand-oriented artists like Jeff Koons and Damien Hirst a run for their money.

However, these top-tier artists who are raking in millions with relative ease remain a minuscule minority. As I have described in previous chapters, the mechanisms of the art market remain steadfastly opaque and tricky to navigate to outsiders – including artists. The problem with the pervasive theory that artists are broke but satisfied to be creative is that no one dares talk about making a living for fear of not seeming committed enough to their art. Even those who have benefitted from a formal art-school education will often struggle with the business of art, which is not a core part of art programmes (if it is taught at all). It is no wonder that so many artists battle with how to create an infrastructure around something as sensitive and esoteric as making art, especially if they feel that it is frowned upon. We have to remember that being an artist is not the same as joining a religious order where one must give up worldly possessions and sublimate desire. There is nothing noble about being broke, and to be an artist is to be a crucial and contributing member of society.

The other issue that affects an artist's ability to improve their financial situation is some kind of unspoken agreement that everyone else is doing better than them. Instead of feeling this way, I want to encourage artists to recognise two things, which, although contradictory, can both be true at once. First, there is a lot of luck involved in being a financially successful artist, because it is impossible to control external factors such as aesthetic trends, shifts in the art market, beneficial geographical conditions, and so on. Second, an artist can – and should – actively build a consistent business around their practice, which endeavours to give them security, a growing profile, and a confidence in their work. You might not be able to control the art market or make a top collector see your work, but there are very real things you can master that will help you to make a living from your artwork.

REMEMBER : YOU ARE A SMALL BUSINESS

Being a professional artist is the same as running a small business. It ain't glamorous and doesn't bring to mind the stereotype of a lovely light-filled Parisian studio, but it's true. Let's burst the bubble further. In this business, the artist is the producer but also often the salesperson, the content creator, the accountant, the technician, the delivery driver, the database manager, the studio cleaner, the social media manager, the catering manager, the public relations person, and the HR department. The artist might not be very competent at a lot of these tasks, especially at first, but nonetheless to make a living from their work they must acknowledge that they exist and begin to build strategies for them.

I heard the hugely successful Grayson Perry give a speech at the British Museum when he had just started to become well known. He said that he'd prepared for success by acknowledging early on that 'being an artist is 20 per cent creativity and 80 per cent the hard graft of turning up every day to do the jobs that needed to be done.' Again, this is not sexy. But it needs to be talked about more, not just to reassure artists that they are not alone, but to make it more widely appreciated that artists deserve proper compensation and support for the work that they do. Let's do away with the myth of the artist pacing the floor with a cigarette as they paint their muse only to put down tools at noon and head to Soho for a long boozy lunch. (Yes, this is more or less the 1960s biography of the artist Francis Bacon, but it's very much out of date.)

THE INVENTORY

A crucial step is to put down a solid administrative foundation upon which to build, which means creating an inventory or archive of your artwork. This might feel daft at first when you are just knocking around in your spare room with some collages. But if you are committed to making a living from your art, you must treat your own work with the seriousness you expect others to treat it with. It is also important to back yourself from the outset and be hopeful for things to come. As Theaster Gates put it, 'When I was broke, I needed hope as currency. I needed to know that even though I didn't have very much, this work that I was doing was very important.' Your work should be important, even if it's just to you, so take care of it and, more specifically, document it. The sooner an artist does this, the better, because if you leave it too late you'll end up with missing information all over the shop.

Much like a collector's inventory, every work needs a title (or inventory number if you are going to call them all 'untitled' – if you were Vincent van Gogh, you might use VVG001, VVG002, and so on). Each work needs to be photographed. Being able to take excellent images of your work is a huge part of the business of being an artist. Take the time to follow tutorials (you'll find some on YouTube) and equip yourself with the skills, as it will not only foster more sales down the line, but it will also save a small fortune on professional photography. You need complete measurements of the work: length, height, and depth. Include a full list of the materials, such as 'oil on linen', or 'mixed media collage including newspaper, yoghurt pot lids, and string'. Record the year it was made – if it took a long time, it's customary to write, for example, 2022–24. If you are making an edition, you need to keep track of the edition number, which has to be set upon release (and never increased), along with the number of artist's proofs, which should always be much lower in number than the edition (for example, an edition of fifty could have three APs). These are for the artist to keep – even though it's your artwork, you can't reprint once you set the edition number. You may sell them later after the edition sells out, usually for a higher price point. You can also donate them to charity exhibitions or try to place them with museums. But always keep one of every work.

SALES RECORDS

The next step of the inventory is to record sales. This should be done with an invoice for every item that includes the full artwork information and date of sale, plus the full name and address of the person acquiring the work. Also include payment terms (such as 'due within fourteen days of receiving this invoice'), because you then have recourse if the client takes too long to pay and you have a chance to sell to someone else. In addition to the invoice (or instead of an invoice, if you gifted the artwork to a friend or charity auction), you should update your inventory with the details of the person who now owns the artwork.

Keeping a record of who owns which work is not just sensible admin – it's potentially critical to future sales down the line. As I described in the chapter on buying art, this is not an ordinary transaction. When I buy a sofa, I don't have much of an emotional connection to the company that sold it to me; after it's delivered, I might never think of them again. An artwork, on the other hand, always feels related to the artist who made it. Buying art is rarely a straightforward matter: it's more often a commitment, an emotional gesture, and many collectors love to stay connected with the artist, even if just watching silently from a distance. Everyone who buys your work is a custodian of something you created, and may talk about your piece – they act as unofficial spokespeople, creating potential future links for your career. So, never lose sight of these people, and make sure you collect their contact details (with their permission), because they are part of your story now. Also, by noting in what month the artworks sold, you can track your business patterns over time. As things develop, it will be possible to see that December is stronger than June for you, or vice versa, which can help you plot activities such as holidays (crucial!).

ONLINE SALES

So, how do sales actually happen? That's the key question and it doesn't have a single answer. Although it might feel completely bewildering, there are things that every artist can do to create opportunities for people to view and acquire their work. First, identify the various 'shopfronts' that are available to you. The internet is going to be a huge part of this picture. Create an easy-to-navigate and simply designed website. It really doesn't have to be a complex matrix: all you need is a gallery or portfolio section with excellent images (if you don't have a great image, don't include it), an artist statement (see page 281), and a contact page with a link to your social media. You can help the visibility of your website by including blog posts to index your site on Google so that the search engine will find it more 'relevant'. The exception to this simple less-is-more approach is websites for digital artists who make

AI- or internet-based art, whose websites may well be intrinsically connected to their practice.

SOCIAL MEDIA

A website is great, but you have to drive traffic to it. Instagram is the go-to platform for artists, with TikTok in second place. It might not feel easy to get Instagram right at first. Many artists ask me how much it should be their personal life and how much their practice. Although some artists have separate profiles, increasingly it makes sense to merge them together. If this is going to be your primary sales vehicle, you need to be clear about individual works: post them separately, with key information such as title, size, and year. Unless it's an Artist Support Pledge work (see page 222), new edition, or a special endeavour such as a charity sale, most artists do not post prices on Instagram and instead write something like 'DM me for details', which pre-social media was known as 'price on application'. This is partly a hangover from the fear of appearing transactional and partly because it lends privacy to an artist's sale prices; some also argue that it encourages conversation. However, I'd like to see a rethink of this approach because ultimately it only adds to the opaque nature of the art world.

Use keywords in the caption and hashtags that are appropriate to your work to help with reach and engagement. Work-in-progress reels or time-lapse videos of new work being created drive enormous amounts of new traffic and followers – the algorithm will reward you for feeding it snackable art content. I appreciate that this is not going to suit everyone, but it is nevertheless where we are. Remember that selling art is a slow business and for every hundred people who look at your work or even like it, you might receive only one enquiry. Don't be disheartened, keep making the work, push yourself forwards and, with consistency, the numbers will improve.

STUDIO SALES

A useful strategy in any sales endeavour is to create a limited time window to motivate action.

You can have a studio sale – whether you physically welcome people into your studio or not (after all, the studio may be your kitchen table but if you do the sale on Instagram, this doesn't matter). You might want to save the sale for a month when sales are slower. You don't need to over-explain it, and you are not undermining yourself – people love a sale (Zara doesn't need to tell me why these shorts are now $15). Let everyone know in advance the start and end date to build anticipation, and provide an insight into what they might expect, such as 'some pieces 50% reduction'. Post excellent images of the works you are putting up for sale, with the full artwork details and both the original and reduced prices. Some artists build pages on their website for the sale, which is only accessible via a password to add privacy, but I suspect that those who are less discreet make more sales.

I would avoid the following: discounts of more than 50 per cent, making too much work available (I'd suggest a minimum of five pieces and a maximum of twenty), and organising the sale just before a big exhibition that you will also want to promote on the same platform, as you may diminish sales of full-price work. You can, of course, have a real-life studio sale if you have a suitable space that can also be promoted and hosted online simultaneously. If you are in a studio block, join forces with your fellow residents to create an open studio weekend.

GALLERY REPRESENTATION

So far, I've talked about a fairly transactional route to selling art – the internet. Although it certainly constitutes the largest proportion of art sales (even major galleries usually sell their work via PDFs and email exchanges, and many auction items are bought sight unseen), it is by no means the most nourishing or exciting way to either sell or buy art. What artists really want is an in-person exhibition – a chance to show a body of work and see their practice in depth.

An exhibition in a gallery is the holy grail for an artist and something that many will struggle to achieve for years, or even decades. Commercial galleries can only work with so many artists at once. They represent a modest 'stable' of artists, and build the careers of those artists over a long time, usually giving each artist a solo show or place in a group show around every eighteen months or two years. Therefore, the number of artists they can exhibit will be limited to between fifteen and thirty, except for the mega galleries, who have multiple spaces and sometimes represent as many as 100 names. Taking on an artist is time-intensive and requires a financial commitment (the rent for the exhibition duration, usually paying for framing upfront, and expenses related to promoting the show), which is why galleries will usually wait for artists to build their own profile before working with them.

If you have a well-developed practice and a track record of sales, then it's certainly worth trying to build relationships with commercial galleries. A gallery will always be more responsive if an introduction is made via a client of the gallery or an artist they work with. This is why so many artists don't just build their online presence, they build their real-world presence by attending gallery private views, museum exhibitions, art fairs, and other events that are opportunities to meet people. A gallery will rarely respond to a cold call (like an email or an unscheduled visit) – they see it as a faux pas to approach them while they are in the middle of an art opening for another artist or, even worse, on the stand at an art fair that has cost them a small fortune and where they must dedicate their time to potential sales. It's hard to hear, but building relationships with galleries will take a lot of time, patience, and very good manners.

OPEN-CALL EXHIBITIONS AND COMPETITIONS

There are, however, many other routes to exhibiting your work and open-call exhibitions are a fantastic place to put your energy. There are websites that list hundreds of open-call exhibitions globally, such as ArtsHub and ArtRabbit.

CREATE YOUR OWN OPPORTUNITIES

You can also create your own exhibition opportunities, such as in a communal space in your studio building or by finding local community spaces, such as libraries, cafes, private members' clubs, pavilions, schools, and even hospitals. There is strength in numbers, so it's worth banding together with other artists to share the organisation of the event and to offer support. This way you can also share your potential audience (for more on the importance of having artist friends, see page 289). Many established organisations started out as a ramshackle grouping together of artists to show their work, such as Urban Art. If you are in a position to make more of a financial commitment, then I would also recommend exploring the Other Art Fair, which is unique in that it offers the chance for artists to exhibit their own artwork at an established fair held in several locations globally that attracts thousands of visitors (see page 221). Again, fellow artists are your friends here, and will gladly share vital intelligence about the fair, such as what to show, how to deal with shipping, and so on. If you don't know any exhibiting artists, ask the fair director to connect you to one – the Other Art Fair has a very collegiate vibe.

ART RESIDENCIES

As well as applying for open-call exhibitions and competitions, it's worth considering applying for art residencies. These intense bursts of time spent making art – often in peaceful surroundings – are a useful way to push your practice forwards and they may come with some form of tuition and a chance to meet other creatives. Beyond the usefulness to your practice, they also offer a kind of badge of honour – you are committed to your work and furthermore were selected for a residency. This all helps to build your reputation and profile and is a solid addition to your CV (see page 281). There are many fully funded residencies, which are naturally harder to get in to, but making these applications is a good discipline. You will be able to use much of the same information to apply to arts funding programmes too. Both art funding schemes and residencies are listed online on websites such as Res Artis.

SIDE HUSTLES

If you speak to an older artist, they will tell you about the pre-digital era, when dinosaurs roamed the earth and artists routinely had a second job to pay the bills. Making money as a contemporary artist is a relatively new phenomenon. Most artists in the twentieth century who didn't get gallery representation didn't have any other opportunities available to them. Many were art teachers, like the German artist Joseph Beuys, who even said, 'To be a teacher is my greatest work of art.' Phyllida Barlow taught at the Slade School of Fine Art for decades, and I love that one of her students, Martin Creed (he of the lightbulbs fame; see page 84), said she was 'the best teacher who never taught him'. The American artist Faith Ringgold taught children art in New York's public schools for twenty years before finally reaching superstar status in the art world.

Others have been art technicians or studio assistants, such as the British painter Rachel Howard who worked for Damien Hirst, or New York-based painter Elizabeth Peyton who worked for the American critic and artist Ronald Jones. Many were commercial artists, like Andy Warhol who made shoe illustrations for advertising, Gerhard Richter (now one of the most expensive living artists) who painted theatre sets, or the Pop artist James Rosenquist, who was a sign painter. Plenty have worked in museums or galleries as wardens, guides, receptionists, or security guards – even the very biggest names like Louise Bourgeois, Damien Hirst, Jeff Koons, and Cindy Sherman.

Finding art-world-adjacent jobs like these can help your practice (think also about working in a framing business, as a graphic designer, or being a commercial photographer or picture editor), but don't forget that many artists had any old side hustle to pay the bills. The American artist Agnes Martin and the Ethiopian-American contemporary artist Julie Mehretu were both waitresses. I hope that these examples reassure you that having a regular or semi-regular source of income outside your art practice does not make you any less of an artist.

BARTER ECONOMY

One other means of supporting your practice is the good old-fashioned barter economy. For example, if you are a photographer, you can offer your skills in exchange for something you need help with, such as delivering artwork or moving studio. Is there a tax accountant who would trade a portrait commission of her kids for advice on setting up a limited company? Perhaps one of the most striking cases of working with no money changing hands is the 2005 case of American artist and actor David Choe, who spray-painted a mural at a young tech start-up in exchange for shares in the fledgling company. He ended up having a $200 million stake in Facebook, which is nice work if you can get it.

You can not only barter skills, you can also trade artworks with other artists, which has happened for centuries. Renaissance artists often sent beautiful drawings as gifts and received one in return. It's a mark of respect to have an artist you admire want to own your work, and when they do, they help to create more audiences for your practice.

KEEP FOCUSED ON THE ART

I know that when you are not selling much (or any) art, it can lead to feeling seriously disheartened, which will threaten to consume your creative energy. Don't lose sight of the fact that being an artist is not all about sales. Put your effort and energy into making artwork that you feel proud of, that is robust, and that satisfies your creative impulses. If you are ever in crisis about all the hats you are wearing in your small business, go back to the work. Keep plugging away at the main endeavour – your art practice. This should always be the priority. You may have to remind yourself of this weekly or daily, because at times it will feel like hard going. Inscribe something on the wall that keeps you focused on the work. I love Maggi Hambling's scrawl on the wall of her studio that reads, 'Stiffen the sinews, summon up the blood', which she borrowed from Shakespeare's *Henry V*.

HOW TO WRITE AN ARTIST STATEMENT

An artist statement is a vital written document. Also known as an artist biography, it is a short overview of an artist's work. Almost every artist I know struggles with writing their statement, because, as the American painter Edward Hopper put so well, 'If you could say it in words there'd be no reason to paint.' Remember that your artist statement doesn't need to explain away the work, which should stand for itself. Instead it should offer a little context or a kind of framework from which to look at an artist's work.

The first thing to grasp when writing an artist statement is that it should be authentic and clear. Don't try to emulate someone else's text or pretend to be something that you are not. Lots of artists make the mistake of using fancy art speak and jargon, because they feel a pressure to conform to a baffling kind of art language. This has become known as International Art English (IAE) – essentially lots of words strung together that say almost nothing and intend to give the impression of a superior language to describe superior art. Words like 'liminal', 'transversal', 'rupture', 'dissonant', and 'collectivity' get thrown around a lot. People are right to be baffled when reading dense texts that use IAE. Clarity is king, so reject IAE!

An artist statement has to be about your work, so take comfort from the fact that it can't be wrong if it's about your work. Keep it clear, concise, and unpretentious – then it will actually be useful. Don't use hyperbolic words or phrases like 'outstanding' or 'one of most esteemed painters of their generation'. These are value judgements that don't belong here – it's not a newspaper review. In essence, try to make this statement the closest you can get to seamless underwear. You want to avoid anyone noticing your artist statement – it should be an invisible device that helps get someone into the art, nothing more.

Here is a breakdown of how to write an artist statement using the example of Vincent van Gogh as if he were still working today. He's my favourite artist and one who has been over-complicated by the media, so he can serve as a useful demonstration of how to keep it simple.

Be consistent in the language, and decide whether you will write in first person ('I am an artist who . . . ') or third person (Vincent van Gogh is an artist who . . . '). If you opt for third person, stick to your surname after the first mention of your full name. To help you make it straightforward, start with simple bullet points and then work these into sentences. It's very helpful to let people know where you were born and where you are based, as well as the year of your birth:

Vincent Van Gogh (b. 1853) is an emerging Dutch painter based in France.

'Emerging' is useful at the start, if it is true, or can be substituted for 'recent graduate' – again, if it is true! Take recent to refer to the past five years. You then need to give a clear and simple overview of what your work looks like and the motivation behind it. Back to Vincent again:

His paintings are characterised by a gestural paint application, which relates closely to his expressive approach to art-making. Deeply committed to nature, van Gogh is an artist who endeavours to communicate how he feels about every scene he depicts. Van Gogh is interested in colour theory and prioritises heightened colour combinations in every picture.

That first paragraph should take people to the heart of the practice, explaining the medium you work in and what the work hopes to achieve. The second paragraph should expand upon the first, ideally with some examples of recent work to demonstrate what you are saying. So, if we go back to my friend, the emerging artist Vincent van Gogh:

While working in the South of France recently, van Gogh painted a series of seven sunflower paintings, treating the traditional subject of floral still lifes with a modern, energetic approach. To the artist, the flowers symbolise gratitude and a vigorous creative life. Normally considered too crude to be a subject in art, van Gogh aims to elevate the sunflower motif in his canvases, to show the flowers in their fullness, going as far as to paint some in the beginning stages of decay.

The third paragraph is optional and should be used to give relevant context on your art career, such as whether you are an art teacher, run or attend any creative programmes, are involved in artist-led spaces, or have participated in any residency programmes. This is the place to put a quotation if you have had any press mentions, or you can ask an influential art-world figure to comment on your work:

Van Gogh is a mostly self-taught artist whose work is informed by his time spent as both a lay preacher and a teacher. In his early twenties, he lived in London, where he was employed by the art dealers Goupil & Cie in Covent Garden, later transferring to the Paris branch. He recently founded an art residency programme called the Yellow House in Arles, which is a space for artists to meet, make work, and exhibit. The first resident was Paul Gauguin in autumn 1888.

The final paragraph should be like a factual list that details education specifics and exhibition history, alongside dates. It doesn't matter if this is short or non-existent at first – what matters is to keep it up to date as things progress. Avoid the generic 'I have work housed in multiple private collections globally', as it is too vague:

Van Gogh was invited to exhibit by Octave Maus in Les XX (18 January–23 February 1890). He participated in the sixth annual exhibition for the Société des Artistes Indépendants (Society of Independent Artists) in Paris (20 March–27 April 1890). He studied drawing at the Brussels Academy in 1880 and was mentored by the Dutch landscape artist Anton Mauve in 1881 in The Hague. He is represented by Theo Van Gogh in Paris and is currently based in Arles.

Despite his staggering fame now, when you write your artist statement, take comfort from the fact that, should van Gogh have written his in his lifetime (such things didn't exist then as it was still so rare to make a living from being a contemporary artist), the final paragraph would document only two group exhibitions (in one of these he sold the only work in his lifetime to a woman collector) and no art degrees. You might not have a list of shows and education as long as your arm, but that doesn't mean you are not an artist.

I MAKE ART AND YOU YOU SAY IT IS AWFUL BUT STILL I I MAKE ART

HOW TO STAY MOTIVATED

There is an awful lot to think about when you are an artist, so much to worry about getting right, not to mention keeping your practice fertile and engaging. As Louise Bourgeois said, 'It is not so much where my motivation comes from but rather how it manages to survive.' I think she gets at something critical here, which is that artists are naturally motivated to make art. But, inevitably, internal or external sources will dampen the desire. Like a small flame, motivation must be protected from being extinguished. And at times, it can even be encouraged to grow into a furnace of energy. What follow in this chapter are some words of encouragement about motivation, from inspiration to self-discipline.

ACCEPT THE CREATIVE CYCLE

Creativity is not a tap that can be turned on and off. It will ebb and flow, catching you off guard. Artistic endeavours are never going to be constant or pre-dictable, and to be an artist is to accept this and the corresponding effect it has on your motivation. You will have to wrestle with the disconnect between what you thought you were going to create and what you actually created. Sometimes this is a pleasant surprise, and you can marshal the unexpected into a new direction or interesting passage in a painting. At other times, it feels like nothing short of failing.

Although this may sound negative, to fail is nonetheless an enormous part of being an artist. Making is learning and remaking is learning again, in an endless cycle. It's helpful to accept that your artistic endeavours will have a cyclical nature and will never run in a straight line. Just because you are not where you intended to be with a work of art, it does not necessarily follow that you are in the wrong place. James Rosenquist expressed this brilliantly, saying that being an artist was 'working like hell towards something you know nothing about'.

NOT MAKING IS PART OF THE PROCESS

At one of my annual Soho House art collection lunches that I host with dozens of artists, I pulled up a chair to join an animated conversation. There was so much passion at play in this group that I couldn't wait to hear what the subject was. I laughed when I realised it was examples of how they all wasted time in the studio. It was clearly a form of catharsis to unload all the ways in which they were *not* producing art, and there was a daftness that underpinned the whole exchange – as if they were trying to outdo one another with their procrastination skills.

But this is the thing: procrastination can actually be a skill – it is a healthy part of the creative process.

Walking the dog for a third time, making copious amounts of tea, trimming fingernails, watering the plants, fooling about on the guitar (which is London-based Tai Shan Schierenberg's go-to) all offer a vital break from the focus that art-making requires. Try to think of procrastination like a visiting relative, though: there should always be an end date to their stay.

CREATE A NETWORK

This artist lunch anecdote touches upon something that I think is fundamental and for which sadly there is no formal network: artists need to be friends with other artists. This is fairly easy to achieve if you are an art school graduate or a based in a busy studio block. Otherwise, it's certainly worth putting some effort into, as it can be an isolating experience to be an artist. It's so useful to be able to share not just practical advice but also to give and receive emotional support. Spending time with a fellow artist, even if your practices are worlds apart, is especially helpful if you are struggling to stay motivated and need an injection of energy.

NURTURE SELF-DISCIPLINE

Picasso said that an artist should 'only put off until tomorrow what you are willing to die having left undone' – which is a tad dramatic, to say the least. Most artists will constantly have to leave an artwork before they want to because of necessary things to attend to such as childcare or domestic responsibilities (two things that Picasso was not famed for). Leaving mid-endeavour might actually help with motivation as there is something pressing to pick back up. I know it certainly helps me when I am writing or curating to leave things in mid-air; I practically race back the next day to finish the job. This is a way of cultivating self-discipline. We don't have to go all macho like Picasso and let nothing stand in the way of our making. Instead, gently tease out strategies that allow the creative juices to spill into the next session.

SEEK INSPIRATION

When you hit a dry patch in your creative endeavours, it will help if you have already worked out some feel-good activities and mechanisms by which you can find inspiration. Some artists might visit their favourite art gallery, whereas for others this will only compound their frustration (the British artist Charming Baker once told me that he feels physically sick if he sees a work by an Old Master while he is struggling with his own painting, so he only goes to the National Gallery when he is on a break from working).

Consuming an alternative form of art, such as literature, film, music, or fashion could help. It might also be enough to simply be with your work but not to make anything. One of the most successful living artists, Peter Doig, learned this at art school and it has always stayed with him: 'One teacher said, "You know, Peter, you don't have to go to the studio only to paint." It's good to look. Sometimes I spend a lot of time there just looking at things.'

SET GOALS

Setting over-arching goals or a strategy for the year ahead is a useful framework, because it allows you to see each day as part of a whole, one cog in a big machine. It might help to step outside your own head-space and escape the immediate moment of boredom, frustration, despondency, or creative block. Every January you could map out some key points in the year ahead – so deadlines for various open-call exhibitions or when you might have a studio sale. You could plot your own DIY art residency by committing to making art with the absolute minimum of distractions every day for one week (treat yourself to an out-of-office email response – if it's urgent, someone will call you). Start to put anchors in, they will help keep you motivated throughout the year. One goal every artist should set is to believe in their work, no matter what obstacles they face. As Tracey Emin puts it, 'The only person who can define your worth is yourself.'

FINALLY MAKE YOUR WORK YOUR BEST FRIEND

Maggi Hambling is a very quotable artist. I have heard her say this sentence so many times I can relay it word for word, but it never fails to make me smile. I think it can be applied more universally beyond the art world, because there is something within it which relates to self-dependency, overcoming problems, and finding release: 'If you're going to be an artist, you have to make your art your best friend – so whatever you're feeling, you can go to it. If you're tired, bored, happy, randy, or sad, you go to your work and have a conversation.'

I love the sentiment that art will always be there with you. Even if you are in crisis, your art is there by your side. This is true for artists and non-artists alike – another beautiful and reassuring thing we can all learn from artists and art.

ONE THING EVERYONE CAN TAKE AWAY FROM THIS BOOK

Art is for everybody. It is an inherent part of human culture the world over, and has been for thousands of years. Art takes us just as we are. It values our individual opinions and emotional responses, and can offer healing, solace, inspiration, exhilaration, and reassurance. Art is yours for the taking, so please, go and take it on your own terms.

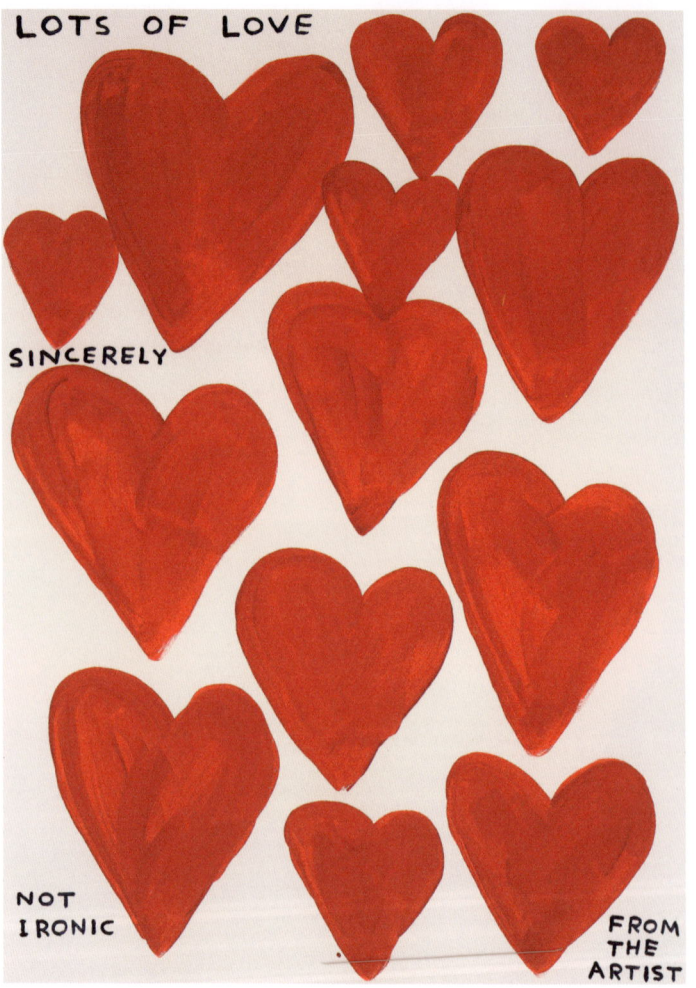

AFTERWORD

How to Art has been nothing short of a passion project. It was a far harder book to write than I could have imagined, because I had to unlearn lots of things, like believing that expensive art is 'better'. I also had to figure out how to unpick the structure of the art world that I have made myself a part of for twenty years. I also sometimes felt a wave of anxiety that I was making myself look very uncool in a world where being cool matters, or that maybe I was somehow betraying my industry and letting the side down. But I reminded myself that I was writing this book about art because I love it so much, and because I believe in it. Because without art, I really don't know what we are all doing here. Art helps us to find meaning, gives our lives depth and beauty, and provides gentle ways for us to connect with one another. So, I'd like to say a heartfelt thank you for taking this journey with me. I really believe that through art we are able to communicate what it is to be human across time and space. In our divided world, this seems more urgent than ever.

WHAT NOT TO SAY TO AN ARTIST

Now that you are attending exhibitions, open studios, and art fairs, you will start to encounter real-life artists. Because of anxiety around the 'codes' of the art world, it's natural to get a bit tongue-tied around them, and possibly even to say a few things that generate a slightly surly response! Artists are sensitive creatures, and I have learned over the years (usually the hard way) that there are some things to avoid saying. So, to improve your art chat, here are some things not to say, with suggestions of a more diplomatic way of phrasing them instead.

YOUR WORK IS EXACTLY LIKE X'S WORK

Originality is of fundamental importance to artists. Better would be, 'I see something of X in your work – are they an inspiration for you?'

THIS LOOKS LIKE IT DIDN'T TAKE VERY LONG

The implication here is that the artist has phoned it in. Instead, try saying, 'It has such a fresh/energetic/ spontaneous quality to it.'

HAVE YOU BEEN ABLE TO SELL NY OF THESE ?

Just say, 'How has the work been received?'

WHERE DID YOU GO TO ART SCHOOL ?

This could insult a lot of people who didn't go to art school. Instead, ask: 'What has been your route into making art?'

AM I SUPPOSED TO SEE SOMETHING ?

When referring to an abstract painting, a gentler thing to ask is, 'What are your inspirations?'

HMMM

Silence or grunting might be your strategy when you don't know how to express what you are thinking, but it could be read as indifference. Instead, either be honest and try, 'I am not sure how to express what I think,' or move the discussion away from the work by asking something like, 'Are many of your friends artists?'

MY FIVE - YEAR-OLD COULD HAVE DONE THAT

Ah, this old classic! Just say, 'It's deceptively simple and has a really great energy.'

I JUST REALLY DON'T GET THIS MODERN STUFF

Why not ask, 'I'd love to get my head around this, can you talk me through it?'

I GET THE PICTURE

JUST BRUSH OFF YOUR CRITICS

CANVAS SOME OPINIONS ON YOUR PAINTING

Puns are probably best avoided. I'm talking to you, Dad.

I LIKE IT BUT WOULD PREFER IT IN BLUE. LET ME SHOW YOU A PICTURE OF MY SOFA

It would probably be best to just stop talking for a bit.

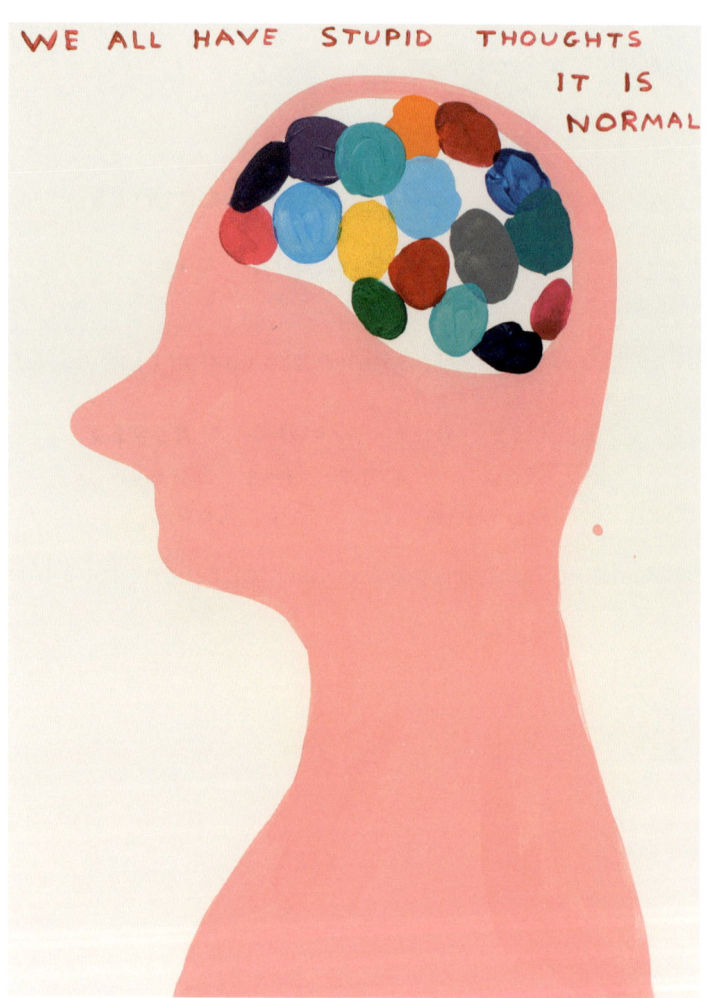

HOW TO AVOID POISONING YOUR CAREER AS AN ARTIST

I hosted an 'ask me anything' talk recently, and a young artist in the audience asked me a razor-sharp question. Instead of the usual, 'What shall I do to get ahead?' or 'How do you get your career going as a young artist?', his question was, 'If I wanted to destroy my career before it even got going, what's the quickest way for me to annihilate everything?'

The inherent playfulness in the question granted me permission to sidestep social niceties about avoiding hurt feelings. I didn't have to add caveats for differing circumstances and exceptions to the rules. I could just plough a mental furrow in which we were both hellbent on ruining his career. Here are the mischievous morsels of career poison I offered up. To my sensitive readers (all the artists), please note that none of these symptoms are terminal – everyone makes missteps and you can always row back. And, to help you do so, I offer the antidotes afterwards.

THE POISON

Complain about other artists' work

Preferably a contemporary who has been signed by a gallery. Artists should allow their jealousy to consume a lot of their working hours, its toxicity maybe even making their own work less focused and original. The real icing on the cake would be to audibly dampen the success of someone who is from a less privileged position and fail to see what they might be able to teach you about working harder, sharpening what you are trying to say, and being more sure of your place.

Price your work very high

Let's suppose that you're in the first two years of your practice. Price a medium-sized painting that took a week to make at $20,000, even though you are without gallery representation, your audience is still small, you have no institutional accolades, and have limited experience. You are suddenly an expensive artist!

Play fast and loose with editions

Make a digital print, silkscreen, or other multiple artwork. Don't worry too much about *how many* are in the edition, just keep selling them for as much as you can until people inevitably realise and overnight all of them will become worthless.

Make sure everyone sees 'SOLD' everywhere in red
Your website is a great place to add large 'SOLD' motifs so that no one can enjoy the artwork and learn about it because they are so busy being told it is SOLD. The added benefit of this is that people will never enquire about sold work and so you'll have fewer potential clients to talk to.

Add big fat signatures to your work
Preferably with a logo, on the front of the artwork. You have just created another world, conjured a visual language, but just so people know the work is something of a commodity, you should mark the territory a bit like an insistent dog.

Be rude and ungrateful to everyone
Adopting a bad attitude because you think it makes you cool and seem hard to get will make people quickly turn their backs.

Ouch.

THE ANTIDOTES

Support other artists
You are all in this together. Someone else being successful does not equate to you failing. Share opportunities, studio space, resources, and encouragement. This act of generosity will help to grow your confidence, plus it's contagious and you will get it back. If you are struggling with the bitter pill of someone

else's achievement, be conscious of how it is affecting your work, and remember that competition is no bad thing if harnessed correctly. Analyse what it is about their accomplishment that grates, then reframe it to help concentrate your own endeavours. It is comforting to remember that often when one artist moves forwards, they create more space for others to follow in their wake.

Be consistent with your prices and allow them to grow with your career

I want artists to be able to make a living from their work, but that means creating a long-term strategy. There is no shame in having a reliable income stream alongside your art career. If you start by pricing your work too high, you can back yourself into a corner that can take years to get out of – you can't lower your prices once they are set. The art world operates on trust, and it is important to take this very seriously as your reputation depends upon it. So, once your prices are set, you should stick to them, but you can operate a 25 per cent friends and family discount or have studio sales periodically.

Be strict with editions

You have to set the exact number of a multiple upon its release. Make the number available too high, and it will be less desirable and could take a long time to sell out, further reducing the appeal. It is far better to play it safe with a lower edition number – if it sells out fast, that's a champagne problem. You are creating more demand and can release more work to satisfy that.

Make your prices available in a sensitive fashion
For a long time, it was an absolute no-no to have prices on your website or Instagram page. The brilliant Artist Support Pledge initiative changed that (see page 222). Once the public saw work clearly marked as available for $200, they bought it in droves. I actively want to be part of a world that allows greater visibility within the art world, and that means we all need to be part of a new area of openness. However, as we straddle the old order, in which listing prices publicly is deemed tacky, we need to be sensitive. A great option is to create an area on your website that explains price points and how to get in touch to discuss them in more detail. 'SOLD' signs are barriers to conversations rather than symbols of your success.

Sign on the reverse or use certificates of authenticity
You need your work to speak for itself, whether it's a photograph, a painting, a ceramic, or a tapestry. A shop-bought cake looks so much more appetising when you take it out of the packaging and put it on a plate. In the same way, most of the time a large signature – which is the packaging, not the art – detracts from rather than adds to a work. Sign small or on the 'unseen' part of the artwork, and create a certificate of authenticity to own alongside the original.

Be nice

I'd love to tell you that all the world's most successful and rich artists are absolute charmers. Sadly, in my experience more than a few of them are ruthless and selfish. The art world does not have to be a popularity contest, but it could do with far greater collaboration and generosity of spirit. Be part of this change, like my friend David Shrigley, who puts his heart into everything he takes on and is a top bloke.

GLOSSARY - SOME USEFUL ART TERMS

This is not a comprehensive list of art terms. Rather it is a selection of words that I think are beautiful or useful to understand.

ABSTRACT ART

Any work of art that does not aim to represent something from the real world in a literal or identifiable way. Instead, it uses shape, colour, form, gestures, lines, and space to convey a feeling or sensation – a bit like the difference between a pop song where you recognise the words and a classical or instrumental piece of music. My favourite abstract artists are the American painter Joan Mitchell and the British sculptor Barbara Hepworth.

APPROPRIATION

Appropriation in art means to use a pre-existing image or object and put it into a new work. This might be someone else's art – for example Andy Warhol's 'remake' of the *Mona Lisa* – or imagery taken from mass culture, such as Warhol's *Campbell's Soup Can* works. Picasso set the stage for appropriation nicely when he (allegedly) said, 'Good artists borrow, great artists steal.'

AVANT-GARDE

A French term that translates as 'advance guard', refer-ring to those in the military who lead the pack. In art, 'avant-garde' relates to any kind of art that is ahead of its time, so work that is pioneering, experimental, and cutting edge. Picasso was a major symbol of the avant-garde for most of the twentieth century but there were plenty of avant-garde women, such as Hannah Höch, who changed art history outside of the limelight.

CHIAROSCURO

An Italian word that, when translated, means 'light-dark'. Chiaroscuro describes a painting technique where passages of dark and light are strongly con-trasted against each other, a bit like seeing a spotlit singer on a stage. For my money, no one uses chiaro-scuro better than the Italian artist Caravaggio, whose paintings appeared cinematic centuries before the advent of film.

CONCEPTUAL ART

A type of art that prioritises ideas over the physical act of making. Concerns about technique, how something looks, or how it is presented are secondary. Conceptual art emerged as a movement in the 1960s and de-emphasised the act of making. Many conceptual works are not made by the artist. Rather, the artist is more like the director of a film, who doesn't necessarily act, write the script, set up the lights, or shoot the footage but is responsible for the overall vision and ensures that everything comes together to achieve it.

CONTRAPPOSTO

Another beautiful Italian word that is used to describe a human figure (painted or sculpted) who stands in a believable pose, usually with a twist to the torso and/or resting their weight on one leg. This dynamic but relaxed stance is in opposition to a front-on, doll-like static posture, which was prevalent before the Renaissance. Next time you pose for a photo, put your weight on your right leg, your right hand on your right hip, and turn your torso slightly left, facing the camera. Congrats, you have gorgeous contrapposto, darling!

EMERGING

'Emerging' in an art context is used to refer to a living artist in the early stages of their career, usually the first ten years. But, as I explain in more detail on page 196, you can be an emerging artist in your sixties after your kids leave home, so it doesn't necessarily mean 'young'. Newer galleries can also be referred to as 'emerging'.

FIGURATIVE

Figurative art or figuration describes art in which there is a recognisable subject – most often an actual human figure – as opposed to abstract art. An artwork does not have to be highly detailed or technically accomplished to be figurative: it is a wide term that includes both Rembrandt's self-portraits and Picasso's Cubist portraits (in both cases we see a human, just in very different figurative styles).

FORMALISM

Formalism is all about the *form* that the art takes: the shape, the colour, the lines, the things that make up the artwork. For hundreds of years, these had been silently employed to create a great effect, but in formalist art they are the subject of the work – the artwork refers to itself more than to the outside world. A good example of this is the Dutch artist Piet Mondrian, who set himself a strict art diet of just a few colours and straight lines. Formalism is also a way of looking at and interpreting art – focusing on the forms as opposed to the narrative or meaning. It's a bit like pulling apart a phone and looking at all its constituent parts rather than considering it as a vehicle for communicating.

FOUND OBJECT

A found object or found art is not that painting you discovered in your aunt's attic. It is a type of art pioneered by Marcel Duchamp in the early twentieth century, whereby an everyday natural or man-made object is transformed into a work of art by the artist. The most famous example is Duchamp's *Fountain* (1917), which was created by taking an ordinary urinal, turning it on its side, and signing it (see page 54). Duchamp changed the course of art history by proposing that an 'ordinary object [could be] elevated to the dignity of a work of art by the mere choice of an artist'.

INSTALLATION ART

Installation art describes art that must be combined with space. Unlike traditional painting or sculpture, the aim is to create something to immerse the viewer in, so they become a more integral part of the artwork and it becomes more of an experience than an object. Tracey Emin's famous work, *My Bed* (1997) is found art, conceptual art, and installation art all at once.

PRIMARY

A description of where an artwork sits in the marketplace. Primary art comes straight from the maker and is being sold for the first time. It becomes secondary after it changes hands. Only living artists can have primary works, since after their death the works will have transferred ownership ... which leads to the next art word, provenance.

PROVENANCE

The history of the ownership an artwork from its creation to the present day. Provenance can tell us the kind of life an artwork has lived: who has treasured it, profited from it, travelled with it, and been influenced by it. Sometimes dealers talk about an artwork having a 'good provenance', which means that the previous owners add some appeal to the work. Everything in the auction of David Bowie's collection, for example, was seen as having a sprinkle of stardust.

REPRESENTATIONAL

Used in the same way as 'figurative' to describe art that represents something from the real world, such as a person, object, or landscape. Again, this is a very wide term – if art is not classed as abstract, then, generally speaking, it is representational. Frida Kahlo's portraits are representational, and so are Johannes Vermeer's domestic interiors, although they are worlds apart in terms of style and history.

SFUMATO

This is my final delightful Italian word. Sfumato, which rhymes with tomato if you're English like me, refers to an atmospheric – or, if literally translated, 'smoked' – painting style where tones and colours are built gradually without any strong outlines. Leonardo was a master at this, creating hazy scenes like his lovely, little-known work, the *Mona Lisa* (see page 117)!

SITE-SPECIFIC

Art that is conceived with a specific space in mind. Like installation art, the space becomes a vital component of the work; the difference here is that the specifics of the exhibition location dictate the nature of the artwork. Emin's installation *My Bed* is not site-specific – it can be shown in multiple locations without changing its meaning. By contrast, Christo and Jeanne-Claude, the late artistic duo celebrated for 'wrapping' buildings and landscapes such as the Arc de Triomphe, made work that could only exist in the space for which it was intended.

STILL LIFE

A genre of art in which the subjects depicted are inanimate objects or without life such as cut fruit and flowers and even, sorry, dead animals. Still lifes may be a way to show off the artist's skill by selecting contrasting textures to paint with a strong lighting source, but they are also usually symbolic, with artists selecting objects that are loaded with meaning – such as apples, which relate to the biblical figures Adam and Eve having a bad day in the Garden of Eden.

VANITAS

Still life leads us nicely to vanitas – a chirpy type of artwork created to remind us of death and the transience of life. Although this is a historic genre, many contemporary artists, such as Cecily Brown and Becky Kolsrud, still pursue it. A skull might be present to do this, but the symbolism might also be insects on food, a burning candle, or a broken object. This is apparently how this book ends: art reminds us that we will be dead one day. Thanks, art!

ACKNOWLEDGEMENTS

I acknowledge and thank every single artist who has ever lived. What you do is magic, and you give my life purpose and meaning. I guess even you, Canaletto.

I would not be writing this book if it were not for people who gave me the confidence to chart my own course and speak my mind in the art world. Aged twenty-two, I was an assistant to Andrew Burnett, then the Deputy Director of the British Museum, who pushed me further than I thought I was allowed to go and was generous enough to forgive what a useless diary keeper I was in light of my fascination for the museum's collection. Other colleagues at the British Museum – namely Patricia Wheatley, Neil MacGregor, and Hugo Chapman – also set me up for life because their vision and passion were so infectious.

In my current position as Chief Art Director at Soho House, I have the great fortune of meeting and working with thousands of artists globally. I am forever grateful to Nick Jones for granting me autonomy and creative freedom in the company he founded.

Thank you to Ben Dunn, my literary agent, who didn't give up until I agreed to throw myself into this endeavour. It's been a hell of a lot of work, but I would do it all over again if it helps people come to art. I'm enormously grateful to my editor, Helen Conford, who lent this book her razor-sharp skills to keep the art-speak at bay and to keep the text accessible and engaging. It's been wonderful to get such warm feedback from everyone at Hutchinson Heinemann and the Penguin Random House family, including Joanna Taylor, Anjali Nathani, Rebecca Ikin, Lydia Weigel, Isabelle Ralphs and Laura Brooke, who all shared their talents with me. I'd also like to thank my U.S. editor Becky Koh and her colleagues Abby Knudsen and Moira Kerrigan, who have been brilliant and supportive about taking the mission across the pond; thank you so much. And thank you to Hayley Gibson for all her help organising the fabulous images.

An enormous fat pile of love and gratitude to David Shrigley, not just for his cover and brilliant artwork throughout the book, but also for being an artist who champions the benefits of art for everyone and makes so many people the world over so happy with his original creations.

Finally, to my family. My parents are legends and endlessly supportive. I know I could not have completed this book without their great love, encouragement, and erm, childcare! I wish for a world where every child has a Nonna and Poppa like you two. Thank you. My spectacular daughter, Juno, has brought me endless joy. Thanks to her, painting is now back to being a regular activity in my life. She has my heart completely and is my favourite person to see art with. And to close, an endless thank you to my husband of 400 years, James. Not only did he read the text several times, he also talked to me at length about parts I found sticky and reassured me like a professional coach when I was shattered . . . which I only occasionally was, since he often makes the dinner and lets me disappear for a crazily hot bath afterwards. You are my hero. All is forgiven on the Canova front.